Twayne's United States Authors Series

Sylvia E. Bowman, *Editor*

INDIANA UNIVERSITY

Gary Snyder

TUSAS 274

Gary Snyder

GARY SNYDER

By BOB STEUDING
Ulster County Community College

TWAYNE PUBLISHERS
A DIVISION OF G. K. HALL & CO., BOSTON

Library of Congress Cataloging in Publication Data

Steuding, Bob.
  Gary Snyder.

  (Twayne's United States authors series; TUSAS
274)
  Bibliography: p. 178–82.
  Includes index.
  1. Snyder, Gary—Criticism and interpretation.
PS3569.N88Z9   811'.5'4 [B]   76-14938
ISBN 0-8057-7174-3

FOR MILES
"Who rules in the mountains, Bear!"

Contents

About the Author

Bob Steuding is an Associate Professor of English at Ulster County Community College at Stone Ridge, New York. He graduated from Siena College in Loudonville, New York, as valedictorian with a Bachelor of Arts in English, and earned his graduate degree from the University of Southern California. He has served on the faculties of the University of Southern California, Chinese University of Hong Kong, Michigan State University, and the Union Graduate School at Antioch College.

Professor Steuding has published articles on Goldsmith, Chaucer, Jeffers, and Snyder; and he has published numerous poems, and also articles about environmental subjects. Recently awarded a Grant-In-Aid from the Research Foundation of the State University of New York, Professor Steuding is presently at work on an historical novel to be entitled "They Took the Heart and Left Us the Rim," and a cycle of poems, "ASHOKAN," dealing with the damming of a river and the inundation of a valley in the Catskill Mountains of New York State, where he lives in an old stone house with his wife and son.

Preface

Since the publication of Jack Kerouac's *The Dharma Bums* (1958) and Gary Snyder's association with the "Beats" of the San Francisco Renaissance, Snyder's prominence as a poet and as a public figure has increased dramatically. Receiving the first flush of favorable and serious criticism in the 1960's for his first two books, *Riprap* (1959) and *Myths & Texts* (1960), from such important poet-critics as James Dickey, Robert Bly, and Kenneth Rexroth, Snyder's poetic reputation is now well established.

Although writing at first in the vein of Ezra Pound and William Carlos Williams and of Oriental nature poetry, the body of Snyder's poetry is not solely Imagistic. His interest in the primitive oral tradition of the American Indian and the obvious impact on his work of poets and writers as diverse as Walt Whitman, Robinson Jeffers, T. S. Eliot, Henry David Thoreau, and D. H. Lawrence attests to this fact. This development from the "crafted" to the "visionary" poem was assured when Snyder, a student of literature and anthropology at Reed College, acquired his lifelong interest in Zen Buddhism. For more than ten years, Snyder pursued these studies in Japan, living for a time in a Zen Buddhist monastery. No poet in American literature has made Buddhist psychology so completely his own. Essentially mystical, Snyder's perception of the oneness of all lifeforms has become a major force in the ecology movement. Outspoken on environmental matters, Snyder addresses himself in his latest book, *Turtle Island* (1974), to the task of learning how we can live and work together on this planet.

No full-length study of the mind and art of Gary Snyder has yet been written. Moreover, Snyder, still in his forties, is at the height of his poetic powers. Thus, a critical work of this sort is doubly difficult to write. Nonetheless, I have attempted to make a start. It is the intent of this "introduction," therefore, to compile information, suggest guidelines, and offer a point of reference whereby one may read with pleasure and understanding the works of this strikingly different poet. In this respect, I anticipate the critical interest in Snyder's poetry which my efforts will hopefully generate.

In this study I have limited myself to a discussion of Snyder as poet, rather than in his other capacities as translator, scholar, and public figure, except where the translations, scholarship, or public activities elucidate the poetry. I have emphasized the poetry while utilizing the prose, especially that collected in *Earth House Hold*, as support. In Chapter 1, I have traced, for those unfamiliar with it, the basic outline of Snyder's life. I have also included additional biographical material in later chapters where pertinent. In Chapters 2 and 3, I have discussed Snyder's style and the significant influences which have shaped it. Chapters 4 through 8 are concerned with an analysis of Snyder's major books of poetry, and the central ideas which engaged his mind and produced each work are traced. Since these conceptions are of continuing interest to Snyder and are found throughout the body of his poetry, an occasional but necessary re-statement occurs. In the final chapter, I have offered a brief discussion of Snyder's reputation, both as a public figure and poet; and I conclude with some tentative comments concerning his contribution to American literature.

This study has not been a solitary enterprise. For cooperation and boundless assistance, and for permission to quote from his works and our correspondence, I am most grateful to Gary Snyder. To senior scholars such as Thomas Parkinson and Kenneth Rexroth, with whom I have not communicated, but from whose pioneering work about Snyder I have benefited immeasurably, and to Linda Wagner, teacher and critic of modern poetry, who first counseled me in this project, I can only express my admiration for their impressive example.

I am also deeply grateful for the generosity and encouragement of my many good friends, such as Dr. Richard Katims, with whom I have rambled in the hills and discussed Snyder, and Joel Bernstein and Dr. Maurice N. Hungiville, a former colleague at Michigan State University who read sections of this book and rendered invaluable critical comment. Furthermore, I would like to express my thanks to the competent staff of The MacDonald De Witt Library at Ulster County Community College, for whom no request was impossible, and to my superlative typist, Mrs. Agnes Miller, who did such an excellent job with the manuscript. And finally, I tender my love and continued admiration to my wife Martha, who courageously took this trip with me into "the back country."

BOB STEUDING

Ulster County Community College
Stone Ridge, New York

Acknowledgments

Quotations from the following works by Gary Snyder are used by permission of New Directions Publishing Corporation: *The Back Country*, copyright 1959, 1966, 1968 by Gary Snyder, reprinted by permission of New Directions Publishing Corporation; *Earth House Hold*, copyright 1957, 1963, 1967, 1968, 1969 by Gary Snyder, reprinted by permission of New Directions Publishing Corporation; *Regarding Wave*, copyright 1968, 1970 by Gary Snyder, "Song of the View," "Song of the Taste," "Song of the Tangle," first published in *Poetry*, reprinted by permission of New Directions Publishing Corporation. Permission has also been granted by New Directions Publishing Corporation to quote from *ABC of Reading* by Ezra Pound, copyright 1934 by Ezra Pound, reprinted by permission of New Directions Publishing Corporation. Permission also granted to quote from "The Wilderness," by Gary Snyder, from *New Directions in Prose and Poetry 23*, copyright 1971 by New Directions Publishing Corporation, reprinted by permission of New Directions Publishing Corporation. Permission also granted to quote excerpts from *Turtle Island* by Gary Snyder, copyright 1974 by Gary Snyder, reprinted by permission of New Direction Publishing Corporation.

Quotations from the following works by Gary Snyder are used by permission of the author and Four Seasons Foundation: *Riprap, and Cold Mountain Poems*, copyright 1958, 1959, 1965 by Gary Snyder, reprinted by permission of the author and Four Seasons Foundation; *Six Sections from Mountains and Rivers Without End*, copyright 1961, 1962, 1964, 1965 by Gary Snyder, reprinted by permission of the author and Four Seasons Foundation; *Six Sections from Mountains and Rivers Without End Plus One*, copyright 1961, 1962, 1964, 1965, 1970 by Gary Snyder, reprinted by permission of the author and Four Seasons Foundation; *Manzanita*, copyright 1972 by Gary Snyder, reprinted by permission of the author and Four Seasons Foundation.

Quotations from *Myths & Texts* by Gary Snyder are used with the permission of Corinth Books, Inc. in association with Totem Press, copyright 1960.

For permission to quote from the following works, I am indebted

Chronology

1930   Gary Snyder, born May 8, 1930 in San Francisco, California. First of two children born to Harold and Lois Snyder.

1932   Family moves to state of Washington.

1942   Moves with his family to Portland, Oregon.

1943–   Enters high school in Portland. Spends summers working at
1945   a camp on Spirit Lake, Washington.

1946–   Works summers for radio station, United Press, and the Port-
1947   land *Oregonian* as a copy boy. Graduates from Lincoln High School, Portland, Oregon. Enrolls in fall at Reed College, Portland, on scholarship.

1948   Summer: ships from New York as galley man.

1950   Publishes first poems in Reed College student publication. Marries Alison Gass. Works summer for Park Service on archaeological site of old Ft. Vancouver.

1951   Graduates from Reed College with degree in anthropology-literature.

1952   Leaves graduate school; returns to San Francisco. Divorces Alison Gass.

1953   Leaves San Francisco and works as lookout on Sourdough Mountain. Works on *Myths & Texts*. Enters University of California at Berkeley, major in Oriental languages.

1954   Works as choker at Camp A of the Warm Springs Lumber Company. Stays until winter shut-down operation. Writes two book reviews for *Midwest Folklore*.

1955   Works on trail crew at Yosemite National Park. Returns to graduate study in Oriental languages at Berkeley. Translates Han-shan. Fall, 1955, meets Allen Ginsberg and Jack Kerouac. Poetry reading given at the Six Gallery in the Marina. Ginsberg reads "Howl." Fall, 1955–Spring, 1956, lives with Kerouac in cabin in Mill Valley.

1956   Leaves for Japan in May to study under scholarship at First Zen Institute of America. Studies Zen and Japanese language.

1957   Leaves Japan and works as a wiper on "Sappa Creek" in the engine room for eight months.

1958   Leaves ship at San Pedrio, California in April. Goes to San Francisco.

1959   *Riprap* published. Returns to Japan for five years.

1960   *Myths & Texts* published. Marries second wife, Joanne Kyger.

1964   Teaches English at the University of California, Berkely. Separates from Joanne Kyger.

1965   *Riprap, & Cold Mountain Poems* and *Mountains and Rivers Without End* (1965). Participates in July, 1965, poetry conference as lecturer and reader. TV tape, *NET*, with Philip Whalen. In October, 1965, returns to Japan to continue his study of Zen Buddhism. Bollingen Grant for 1965–66. Divorced from Joanne Kyger.

1966   *A Range of Poems* published. American Council of Arts and Sciences Prize. Returns to United States. Gives readings on college campuses.

1967   Returns to Japan (March). Lives at Banyan Ashram. Marries Masa Uehara on rim of active volcano.

1968   *The Back Country* published. Son Kai born. Wins Levinson Prize for "Eight Songs of Clouds and Water" (Poetry: 111). Awarded Guggenheim Fellowship. Returns to the United States (December).

1969   *Earth House Hold* published. *Regarding Wave* published in limited edition by The Windhover Press. Son Gen born.

1970   *Regarding Wave* published in expanded edition by New Directions.

1971   Builds home in Sierras. Reads paper, "The Wilderness," at The Center for the Study of Democratic Institutions, Santa Barbara, California.

1972   *Manzanita* published in limited edition by Four Seasons Foundation. Further sections of *Mountains and Rivers Without End* published. Attends United Nations Conference on the Human Environment, Stockholm, Sweden. Returns to Japan in summer to research book on Hokkaido wilderness for Friends of the Earth.

1973   *The Fudo Trilogy* published in limited edition by Shaman Drum. Contains three poems: "Spel Against Demons," "Smokey The Bear Sutra," and "The California Water Plan."

1974   *Turtle Island* published, including "Manzanita" and previously unpublished material.

1975   Awarded Pulitzer Prize for Poetry for *Turtle Island*. First Modern Language Association seminar on poetry of Gary Snyder led by Bob Steuding and Richard Corum, held in San Francisco, December 27.

1976   Continues work on expanded version of prose book on Hokkaido wilderness area of Japan, tentatively to include photographs and essays on ecological topics. Continues work on *Mountains and Rivers Without End*.

CHAPTER 1

Introduction

G ARY Snyder, born under the sign of Taurus the Bull, is a short, tightly-built man who knows his own mind and how to follow its dictates. As a child, during the Depression, life was difficult for Snyder, but he recalls that there were always books in his home and that his mother, to whom he later dedicated *Turtle Island*, read poetry to him at night. Edgar Allan Poe was a particular favorite because of Poe's use of sound, a quality in poetry which continues to interest Snyder. Another early interest, sparked by the woodcraft and natural history books of Ernest Thompson Seton which the young Snyder devoured, was exploring the forests around Portland, Oregon, where he moved with his family about the time he entered high school. Here Snyder developed his attachment to nature and learned self-reliance, discipline, and the rugged ways of the American West, which sustain him to this day, and which frequently appear as the subject matter of his poetry. Also at this time, Snyder obtained his first taste of mountaineering, becoming the youngest member of the noted Mazamas Mountain Climbers. During summer vacations, Snyder worked at a camp in Washington and later on ships at sea. The poems in *Riprap* (1959), his first book, draw on these rugged, virile experiences and explore poetically his youthful adventures.

On his own after the separation of his mother and father, Snyder held many manual jobs before his first poems on the themes of youth and nature were shown to a Reed College professor. Subsequently, Snyder enrolled in the fall of 1947 at Reed with a scholarship, and majored in literature and anthropology. After a weak start, Snyder became quite successful as a student, building a reputation for brilliance and daring which lasts to this day. Some of the credit for Snyder's orientation to formal studies and for his focus on anthropology, especially on Amerindian ethnology, best expressed in his insightful and comprehensive bachelor's thesis "The Dimensions of a Myth," might possibly be attributed to Reed College professor David French. For Snyder took many courses with French, and it was under French that Snyder collected and studied Northwest Coast Indian myths and folktales, the basis of Snyder's second published book, *Myths & Texts* (1960). During his college years, Snyder also married for the first time, worked on an archeological site in Vancouver, and published his first poems in the student publications *Janus* and *Gurgle*. These early poems, published in the period 1950-51, were written about nature, classmates, and mountaineering. "a poem," "Song," "Autumn Equinox," "Senecure for P. Whalen," "For George Leigh Mallory / Missing on Everest," and "By the North Gate, Wind Blows Full of Sand," were Snyder's first excursions into print. Although immature efforts, they indicate his growing awareness of a poetic vocation. However, it was to take Snyder another semester after graduation from Reed to accept the demands of the muse.

After summer work as a timber scaler on the Warm Springs Indian Reservation in Oregon, Snyder left for Indiana University and further study in linguistics and the primitive oral tradition. His interest in spoken language remains important to Snyder and the aural element of his poetry is quite pronounced at times. However, Snyder soon decided that he did not seek the academic or governmental career to which his graduate studies would inevitably lead him. The first poems of *Myths & Texts* and "A Berry Feast," later published in *The Back Country* (1968), make it clear that Snyder's path lay not in the halls of academe, but in the rough-and-tumble world of the Far West. Returning to San Francisco after one semester, and then rooming with a former classmate — the poet and Zen Buddhist Philip Whalen, who was to interest Snyder in Zen and lookout work — Snyder began his tenure as summer forest-fire lookout at Crater Mountain in the State of Washington and later at Sourdough Mountain. This latter locale became the inspiration and setting for one of Snyder's first wilderness poems, "Mid-August at Sourdough Mountain Lookout." Praised by novelist Jack Kerouac, this poem later became the lead poem in Snyder's first book, *Riprap*. An interesting photograph of Snyder appears as the frontispiece in the 1969 edition of *Riprap and Cold Mountain Poems* published by Four Seasons Foundation. In this photograph, Snyder stands in the doorway of his Sourdough lookout, wearing shorts and looking quite jaunty and fit, just as Kerouac, in *The Dharma Bums*, describes the buoyant Snyder portrayed as Japhy Ryder.

Descending from the high country late that summer, Snyder was soon to further his career through his meeting with San Francisco's literary patriarch Kenneth Rexroth. Through his association with Rexroth and Kerouac, and later with the poet Allen Ginsberg, Snyder participated in the now historic poetry reading at the Six Gallery in 1955, a reading in which Ginsberg's poem "Howl" bemoaned the destruction of the "best minds" of his generation. Thus began the movement, later known as the San Francisco Renaissance, which was to affect an all-out attack on American mass culture, reaching the halls of Congress, the Pentagon, and even the university.

Although at this time Snyder lived a seemingly chaotic existence in a Mill Valley cabin with Kerouac, as portrayed in Kerouac's novel *The Dharma Bums*, this was a significant period of work, study, and meditation for Snyder. He had decided what he would do with his life. Thus, he enrolled at the University of California at Berkeley, studying with Professor Ed Schafer in the Department of Oriental Studies — but not working toward a degree — and later with Shih-hsiang, ultimately translating twenty-four of the *Cold Mountain Poems* of Zen hermit poet, Han-shan. These vivid translations smack more of the cold high country of the American West, with which Snyder was then familiar, than of ancient China, but they are an excellent adaptation of Han-shan's poetry to Western sensibility and taste, and they remain great favorites of readers oriented toward mountains and the out-of-doors. Clearly, as Snyder's studies indicate, at this time he had decided, in addition to writing poetry, to become a Buddhist and to study Zen Buddhism in Japan. In 1956, he left for Kyoto, Japan, with a scholarship to study at the First Zen Institute of America. During this time poems and letters describing his travels and his Zen training appeared in American periodicals; yet except for nine months spent in 1958 in San Francisco, another brief stay (1964–65) in which he taught English at Berkeley, made a National Educational Television tape with Philip Whalen, participated in a poetry conference, and gave readings at a number of colleges across the country, Snyder remained for the most part in Japan until December, 1968, when he returned permanently to the United States.

From 1959 until 1964, a period described in "Six Years," and from

1965 until 1966, the date of the death of his teacher Oda Sesso, Snyder lived for the most part in Kyoto. He also worked intermittently on tankers at sea. His marine experiences are described in *Riprap*, which is dedicated to many of the men with whom he worked and by whom he was influenced. After marrying his second wife Joanne Kyger — a short-lived marriage ending in divorce in 1965 — he spent six months (1961–62) traveling with Ginsberg and Peter Orlovsky through India. This experience is captured in "Kali" from *The Back Country*; in "A Journey to Rishikesh and Hardwar" in *Earth House Hold*; and in "Now, India" (*Caterpillar* 19 [October] 1972). During these productive and rewarding years from 1959–1968 Snyder published five books of poetry and obtained numerous grants and awards. In 1967 Snyder married his third wife, a Japanese named Masa Uehara, celebrating the marriage on the rim of an active volcano on Suwa-No-Se Island off the coast of Kyushu, Japan, as described in "Suwa-No-Se Island and the Banyan Ashram," Snyder's essay published in *Earth House Hold* (1969). After the birth of his first son, Kai in 1968, the family left Japan and the Banyan Ashram to set up housekeeping in the United States.

Since this time, as this study will discuss in due course, Snyder's life has changed. Celebrating his new domestic and more settled situation, Snyder published *Regarding Wave* (1969). Then in 1971, disgusted with urban life, Snyder moved from San Francisco to his new home, "Kitkitdizze" (named for a local plant) in the foothills of the Sierra Mountains of California. Deeply concerned with the fate of the environment, Snyder has become an increasingly more outspoken advocate for wilderness and ecological awareness. Far from shunning the media in his effort to restore ecological sanity, Snyder has published in the popular press (magazines such as *Look*) and appeared on numerous campuses across the country. Selected along with poet Michael McClure by the Portola Institute, publishers of the *Whole Earth Catalog*, Snyder attended the "United Nations Conference on the Human Environment" in Stockholm, Sweden in 1972. His report, "Mother Earth," published in poetic form, appeared in the *New York Times* (July 13). In 1973 Snyder continued the publication of ecologically-oriented poetry by issuing *The Fudo Trilogy*, and in 1974 published his latest work, *Turtle Island*, for which he was awarded the Pulitzer Prize for Poetry. *Turtle Island* attempts to restore a sense of reverence and mindfulness regarding our continent, which Snyder points out the Indians called "Turtle

Island," because they believed, quite significantly that man rides on this mythical creature's back.

At present Snyder lives at home with his family and friends. Their goal, remarks Snyder, is greater independence and self-sufficiency. In this regard it is interesting to note that although Snyder's work is widely read and accepted by critics, and although he has become a national celebrity, he still maintains the disciplined pace of his earlier life, continuing his Buddhist studies, planning the translation of a Buddhist manual for Westerners, working toward the creation of a community of Western Buddhists, and, of course, writing poetry. In the period 1975–76 Snyder also progressed with work on *Mountains and Rivers Without End* and continued to compose the ecological essays which will be included in a forthcoming book to be published by Friends of the Earth. Only in his forties, Snyder has yet much to do. And when asked about his past and his feelings about his many accomplishments in his rise from backwoods poverty to notoriety, Snyder characteristically responds, "I never look back."[1]

CHAPTER 2

Developing a Style

I *"an amusing cultivated mind"*

IN a National Educational Television presentation filmed in 1965,
Gary Snyder stated: "My poems are about work, love, death,
and the quest for wisdom. What we have is the ground beneath our
feet, our minds and bodies, the men and women who bore us, the
man or woman we live with, the children we have made, and the
friends we know."[1] Such statements clearly exhibit what Kenneth
Rexroth sees as the basic tendencies of the "New American Poets."[2]
These Rexroth considers to be anti-formalism, re-international-
ization, directness of statement, and presentational immediacy, or
what Rexroth calls "repugnancy for literary cookery."[3] Clearly,
Snyder's style is straight-forward, cross-cultural or eclectic and anti-
academic. In addition, one notes the obvious presence of the poet in
all his work; for his anecdotal element is usually evident. The figure
of Snyder permeates his poetry; for Snyder, a conscious mythmaker,
takes his own advice to sit by the road and hatch new myths.

The basic characteristics of the poems of this "amusing cultivated
mind" are, as Thomas Parkinson states, easy to detect and to imitate, if impossible to duplicate.[4] The elements of a typical Snyder
poem are: (1) a wilderness, or Oriental setting; (2) an avoidance of
abstraction and an emphasis on the concrete; (3) a simple, organic
form, with generally imagistic lines; (4) the use of colloquial language, with the exploitation of oral aspects; (5) esoteric allusion; (6)
occasional erotic overtones. Certain of these more significant
points should be developed in greater detail.

First, the selection of images is the basic organizing device of
Snyder's art. Images are concrete; they are held to objects that are
visual and generally sensuous. In this respect, Snyder is significantly influenced by Oriental poetry, by Ezra Pound, and by
William Carlos Williams' dictum "No ideas but in things." The pre-

sentation of images is usually organized in one of three ways: (1) in a series — a series of perceptions or a multiplication of details around a central image, as in "All Through the Rains"; (2) in a progression — the movement toward or away from the observer in the poem, as in "Kyoto: March"; or (3) in a balance, abstract against concrete, simple against complex.

Second, Snyder's choice of words is sparse and colloquial. As Snyder writes in his journal, "fewer the artifacts, less the words, slowly the life of it / a knack for non-attachment" (*Earth House Hold*, 9). This brevity and concreteness can be seen in his first book, *Riprap*. In "Nooksack Valley" Snyder relates how he is "Caught more on this land — rock tree and man, / Awake than ever before. . . ." Revisiting his old homestead before leaving for Japan in 1956, Snyder describes vividly and sensuously the farm where he once lived in the Northwest:

> the cedar walls
> Smell of our farm-house, half built in '35.
> Clouds sink down the hills
> Coffee is hot again. The dog
> Turns and turns about, stops and sleeps.[5]

Tough, hard diction is also evident in the tanker poems, "The Sappa Creek" and "T-2 Tanker Blues." And in "Above Pate Valley," inspired by work on a trail crew in the high Sierra, Snyder, avoiding abstract philosophizing and rooting himself in the concreteness of the experience, writes:

> Picked up the cold-drill
> Pick, singlejack, and sack
> Of dynamite.
> Ten thousand years. (*Riprap*, 9)

Third, Pound and the Orient taught Snyder to lay down a line. As in Pound and in Chinese poetry, Snyder often uses stress centers rather than the conventional syllables. He couples and halves lines, pausing with a caesura or with a line break that is roughly in the center of the line. Of course, he varies this technique quite frequently. A few lines from "Logging, 14" in *Myths & Texts* should illustrate this point:

> Crosscut and chainsaw
>   squareheads and finns
>   high-lead and cat-skidding
> Trees down
> Creeks choked, trout killed, roads.

The pattern here is 1 - 2 (pause); 1 - 2, 1 - 2 (pause); 1; 1 (pause); 1, 1 - 2, 1 - 2, 1 - 2, 1. Words such as "cat-skidding" and "high-lead" are read as one stress center and not, in each case, as three syllables: cat-skid-ding. Thus, Snyder is able to develop the sense and rhythm of the dogged march of "progress" and its inevitable consequences. "Logging, 3" offers another example of this technique: the rhythm, the pause, and the final variation:

> The cows get thin, the milk tastes funny,
> The kids grow up and go to college
> They don't come back.
>   the little fir-trees do. (*Myths & Texts*, 6)

The fourth characteristic is Snyder's particular use of sound and rhythm. Through his studies of the spoken literature of the American Indian, Snyder became interested in the aural as well as in the visual reception of poetry. He became fascinated with the use of the voice, as in primitive poetry, to delight and to structure art. Snyder was later to define poetry in his essay "Poetry and the Primitive" ". . . as the skilled and inspired use of the voice and language to embody rare and powerful states of mind that are in immediate origin personal to the singer, but at deep levels common to all who listen" (*Earth House Hold*, 117). Like Charles Olson, Snyder understands the relationship of physiology and breathing to poetry. Again, in "Poetry and the Primitive" he writes: "Breath is the outer world coming into one's body. With pulse — the two always harmonizing — the source of our inward sense of rhythm. Breath is spirit, 'inspiration.' Expiration, 'voiced,' makes the signals by which the species connects" (*Earth House Hold*, 123).

Snyder utilizes, therefore, many of the techniques of oral transmission in his poetry. Especially prevalent is the use of primitive narrative techniques such as alliteration, internal rhyme and rhythm, repetition, the inclusion of anecdotes in lyric poems, and the mixing of time sequences and locales, thus developing a timeless and placeless quality. Even Snyder's infrequent use of punctuation may be seen in terms of his greater concern for the aural aspect of poetry. "Bubbs Creek Haircut" in *Mountains and Rivers Without End* employs these narrative techniques admirably. The prose-like or even Hemingwayesque quality of "The Elwha River" in *Mountains and Rivers Without End* is also interesting in this respect. "The poem on the page," is clearly, as Parkinson states, "evidence of a voice. . . ."[6]

Oral elements are used extensively in *Myths & Texts*, a work written under the influence of Snyder's experiences with Indians while studying anthropology at Reed College. The anecdote insert is used in "Logging, 6," "Logging, 10" "Hunting, 12," and "Burning, 8." This work also utilizes the song and the chant, for even animals sing their own songs, as in primitive ritual. In addition, the work, as a whole, makes good use of alliteration, repetition, and other vocal qualities. In "this poem is for bear," for example, Snyder makes effective use of chant and repetition. He writes:

> snare a bear: call him out:
> honey-eater
> forest apple
> light-foot
> Old man in the fur coat, Bear! come out!
> Die of your own choice!
> Grandfather black-food!
> this girl married a bear
> Who rules in the mountains, Bear!
> you have eaten many berries
> you have caught many fish
> you have frightened many people. (*Myths & Texts,* 22)

In the final lines of the poem, the poet employs the surprise ending for humorous effect and comic relief:

> — I think I'll go hunt bears
> 'hunt bears?
> Why shit Snyder,
> You couldn't hit a bear in the ass
> with a handful of rice!' (23)

Clearly, the control of the primitive raconteur is exhibited in this marvelously balanced poem. The ironic contrasts in the final lines serves to heighten the enjoyment of the listener and to increase the intensity of the effect.

II *Riprapping*

Once, when asked how he writes, Snyder responded that watch-fulness was central to his approach to poetry. One must always "hold oneself ready" for inspiration, states Snyder — for what he calls the "voice within." Stating that he composes about fifteen poems a year, writing only the poems he likes, editing in his head first, and omit-ting the inconsequential, Snyder remarks that he maintains the dis-cipline of content and organization. He seeks "what has bones in it": "It's like backpacking. I don't want anything that's unnecessary."[7] This general statement, although frank and interesting, is somewhat misleading in its simplicity. It must be scrutinized carefully; for, although much of Snyder's poetry is, strictly speaking, visionary, it is a highly crafted response to revelation.

In *Earth House Hold,* Snyder sets up this dichotomy between "*Poems* that spring out fully armed; and those that are the result of artisan care. The contrived poem, workmanship; a sense of achievement and pride of craft; but the pure inspiration flow leaves one with a sense of gratitude and wonder, and no sense of 'I did it' — only the Muse" (56–57). He adds that ". . . one shouts for the moon in always insisting on it; and safer-minded poets settle for any muddy flow and refine it as best they can" (57). Also using similar water imagery, Snyder relates in "Civilization,"

> When creeks are full
> The poems flow
> When creeks are down
> We heap stones. (*Regarding Wave,* 84)[8]

As these quotations indicate, fabrication and revelation are closely intertwined in the body of Snyder's poetry. Certainly, Snyder is foremost a hard worker and a meticulous craftsman. From an early age, poetry seems to have been Snyder's *sadhana,* his discipline or ordering task. One can clearly see in his early poems the relation-ship in Snyder's mind between poetry and craft. In "Riprap" he compares the placement of rocks for making trails in the mountains to the writing of poetry:

> Lay down these words
> Before your minds like rocks.
> placed solid, by hands
> In choice of place, set
> Before the body of the mind
> in space and time:
>
> . . .
>
> each rock a word
> a creek-washed stone (*Riprap*, 30)

In this tight unit, poetry is seen as masonry. Each word, like each stone placed to make a trail, is appropriate; it is in the correct position to accomplish its purpose. In keeping with the teachings of that great craftsman Ezra Pound, Snyder's diction is sparse and tough; the concrete images cluster around one particular, the act of riprapping, and are developed through association. Since nothing is left to chance, this poem is carefully wrought. The diction of the poem, like the carefully placed rocks making a trail, enable the reader to ascend, offering sure footing, as Snyder relates in his second book *Myths & Texts*, "on the slick rock of metaphysics" (43).

In this poem, even the words are conceived of in their nature as things, as concrete objects. As when one lays a stone foundation, a bluestone walk, or a patio, each choice is significant and effects the complete design of the finished work. The intricate patterning of riprapping reminds Snyder of the game "go," a Japanese game that is something like a cross between checkers and hopscotch. In this game, the player tosses a stone or similar object consecutively into areas of a figure outlined on the ground and hops through the figure and back to regain the object. As suggested in Snyder's "Hop, Skip and Jump," written for two little friends with whom the poet played hopscotch, this intriguing game sheds light on the more important act of writing poetry. In this game, as in riprapping, stones are "placed solid, by hands / in choice of place, set. . . ." Snyder writes in "Hop, Skip, and Jump,"

> she takes stone,
> with a white quartz band for her lagger.
>
> . . .
>
> he takes a mussel shell . . .
>
> . . .
>
> he is tiny, with a flying run & leap —
> shaggy blond — misses all the laggers. . . . (*The Back Country*, 107)

Later in the poem Snyder writes, "we have all tripped and fallen" (107). Clearly, only the realization that go and hopscotch are games mitigates the sense of seriousness invested in the acts of riprapping and writing of poetry. Of *Riprap* and his approach to poetry at that time, Snyder writes in Donald Allen's *The New American Poetry*:

> *Riprap* is really a class of poems I wrote under the influences of the geology of the Sierra Nevada and the daily trail-crew work of picking up and placing granite stones in tight cobble patterns on hard slab. "What are you doing?" I asked old Roy Marchbanks. — "Riprapping" he said. His selection of natural rocks was perfect — the result looked like dressed stone fitting to hair-edge cracks. Walking, climbing, placing with the hands. I tried writing poems of tough, simple, short words, with complexity far beneath the surface texture.[9]

In addition to his sense of craft and purpose, Snyder's reverence for work and the job to be accomplished is evident in this quotation. Since the vocation of poet was most probably not valued in the rural Northwest where Snyder grew up, he must have considered carefully the validity of becoming a poet. He must have wondered if poeticizing could be considered work. It is not surprising, therefore, to see the "work ethic" rear its head. Also in Allen's anthology, Snyder relates: "I've just recently [1959] come to realize that the rhythms of my poems follow the rhythm of physical work I'm doing and life I'm leading at any given time — which makes the music in my head which creates the line.[10] Clearly, in certain respects Snyder regards poetry as an extension of physical labor.

Some of Snyder's best poetry, especially in his earlier books, is written about his work experiences. Considering himself a worker (he is a member of the National Maritime Union) and dedicating many poems to the men he has worked with and learned from as in *Riprap*, Snyder identifies with the working class rather than with the man of status and position. These sympathies relate to his love of the hobo, the bindle stiff, and the Zen *bihhiku*. As a child, Snyder grew up in a working-class home. With obvious pride, Snyder has stated, "As much as the books I've read the jobs I've had have been significant in shaping me. My sense of body and language and the knowledge that intelligence and insight, sensitivity, awareness, and brilliance are not limited to educated people, or anything like it".[11]

Snyder as poet-worker is responsive to tools. Many of his poems contain references to the tools he uses: the saw, rake, and singlejack hammer. In "The Late Snow and Lumber Strike of the Summer of Fifty-four," he writes about the pools "of cold oil / On back porches of ten thousand split shake houses" (*Riprap*, 2). This is a striking image for anyone who has lived in the Northwest. Logging is one of the major occupations in this rugged, heavily forested part of the country, and the chainsaw with its noise, acrid smell, and dripping oiliness is ever-present. The chainsaw and its fellow, the caterpillar (bulldozer), are true symbols of the West and the Western working man. Thus, when Snyder relates that the loggers are on strike, "all gone fishing," and later adds, mentioning the saw at the lumber mill, "The green-chain still" (2–3), one feels some of the sense of desolation that the man out of work experiences. This image of an idle tool suggests loss of dignity, livelihood, and sustenance. Snyder, fired from the Forest Service in 1954 for supposed but unfounded Communist affiliation, looks for work in the poem; and the reader feels his sense of dependency and powerlessness. He relates, "Hitched north all of Washington / crossing and re-crossing the passes / Blown like dust, no place to work." And he continues,

> I must turn and go back:
> > caught on a snowpeak
> > between heaven and earth
> And stands in line in Seattle.
> Looking for work. (3)

The strong sense of frustration is evident. Even though he travels to majestic Mt. Baker, "In a gully of blazing snow," he is, of necessity, drawn to the "cities down the long valleys west"; for he is "thinking of work."

In "Twelve Hours Out of New York After Twenty-Five Days at Sea" (*The Back Country*, 105), Snyder relates his pride of ownership in the Japanese tools which he brings back to the United States. "Six-Month Song in the Foothills" (*The Back Country*, 17) describes the act of sharpening saws in preparation for work. And in "The Sappa Creek" even the simplest of tools, the rag, is given its due: Snyder relates the many sources and varieties of this tool:

> Rags in bales, the final home for bathrobes,
> Little boy blue jeans and housewife dresses
> Gay print splash-all wiping oil off floorplates,
> Dangling from hip pockets like a scalp. (*Riprap*, 24)

Finally, in "After Work," Snyder venerates the tools which enable him to live. These simple, primitive tools, presented as a list of inanimate, ordinary objects, assume for Snyder, and thus for the reader, unusual significance. Collecting his tools, "the axe, the rake," and entering his cabin for food and love, Snyder elevates these extensions and celebrates his central concern for craft and a job well done. With complete sensitivity to the sacramental, ritualistic nature of his actions, and with total awareness of the importance of this and every moment in his life, the poet states,

> we'll lean on the wall
> against each other
> stew simmering on the fire
> as it grows dark
> > drinking wine (*The Back Country*, 27)

III *"Grope and stutter for the words"*

Although Snyder was soon to develop an individual style, his first poems were essentially traditional. In *Riprap*, one reads lines such as, "Damn me not I make a better fool" (28) and "like thin ice — the sudden / Feel of an old phrase made real. . ." (14). In "Migration of Birds," the early influence of the Western literary tradition is also evident, for Snyder writes, "It started just now with a humming bird," and concludes, "Across the hill the seabirds / Chase Spring north along the coast. . ." (17). The first lines quoted above sound less like Snyder than Milton, whom Snyder, as if aware of cultural indebtedness, criticizes in "Milton by Firelight." In the second quotation, Snyder builds his poem upon the basis of a cliché, a practice considered trite by most contemporary poets.

In these early poems, Snyder is obviously striving for effect. The poems are contrived, worried into existence. The style is traditional; the subject matter, conventional. As Thomas Parkinson indicates, Snyder's work at this early stage is ". . . an uneasy wedding of European forms with attitudes that threaten and try desperately to break those forms."[12] These "attitudes" — ultimately resolved in a "reconciliation of opposites"[13] that was sought unsuccessfully by Yeats, Eliot, and Pound — were soon to lead Snyder to experiment and ultimately to create a poetic synthesis all his own, that was philosophically, a step or two beyond the modernist tradition.

This search for a new form and Snyder's struggle to liberate himself from traditional Western meter, especially rhyme, is seen in a Middle-English quotation from Chaucer's *The Canterbury Tales,* one cited by Snyder in his journals:

> "By God" quod he, for pleynly, at a word
> Thy drasty rhyming is not worth a tord. (*Earth House Hold,* 5)

Of course, Snyder construes the meaning of this quotation differently than the original poet intended. However, realizing the stage in his career at which this statement caught his eye, one can readily understand his sentiment. This desire to kick over the traces and break into new territory can also be seen in *Riprap,* although essentially it is stylistically traditional. "A Stone Garden" offers a good example because one can see in this early poem not only the traditionalisms but the strain against traditional meter and the search for a freer form that are later developed in the elliptical experiments of *Myths & Texts* and in the more complete coalescence of form and content in *Regarding Wave.* In many ways, the poem is the usual, pre-modernist fare. Robert Frost might have written it, if he had studied the simple people of Japan as he did those of New England.

> & walked a hundred nights in summer
> Seeing in open doors and screens
> The thousand postures of all human fond. . . . (*Riprap,* 21)

The poem is constructed upon a single metaphor. Japan is a huge stone garden like rocks placed in the sea. The subject is abstract, even philosophical, and is divided into four sections of about equal length. Symmetrical and orderly, the form is impressed upon the content. Certainly, the poem was written to be read. It is a visual, or graphic experience, pre-McLuhan, different from the oral nature of Snyder's second work *Myths & Texts.* In "A Stone Garden" the lines are regular, often iambic: "I recollect a girl I thought I knew." There are lines which are contrived:

> And I that night prowled Tokyo like a bear
> Tracking the human future
> Of intelligence and despair. (21)

And,

> The oldest and nakedest women more the sweet,
> And saw their first old withered breasts
> Without an inward wail of sorrow and dismay
> Because impermanence and destructiveness of time
>
> In truth means only, lovely women age —
> But with noble glance of I Am Loved
> From children and from crones, time is destroyed. (21–22)

Although in these lines one can see Snyder's growing Buddhism, the diction is particularly abstract and literary. Snyder uses inversion in the line, "more the sweet," and a concluding statement, "time is destroyed," to make a specific point. Sections one and two end with rhyme, and there is frequent use of internal rhyme in the first section. In section three, however, something different occurs; Snyder departs most openly from traditional meter. Although at times rhyme is used and an occasional phrase such as "Flits over yonder hill" appears, the form comes much closer to content. In this section, too, Snyder states his dilemma:

> Thinking about a poem I'll never write.
> With gut on wood and hide, and plucking thumb,
> Grope and stutter for the words, invent a tune,
> In any tongue, this moment one time true
> Be wine or blood or rhythm drives it through —
> A leap of words to things and there it stops. (22)

Although the poem remains held by things, as is the early poetry of William Carlos Williams, and by the language he uses to conceptualize and present the experience, it is evident that Snyder has reached new territory, or at least has shown his awareness of its existence and his desire to attain it. Snyder writes,

> Creating empty caves and tools in shops
> And holy domes, and nothing you can name;
> The long old chorus blowing underfoot
> Makes high wild notes of mountains in the sea.
> O Muse, a goddess gone astray
> Who warms the cow and makes the wise man sane,
> (& even madness gobbles demons down)

> Then dance through jewelled trees & lotus crowns
> For Narahito's lover, the crying plover,
> For babies grown and childhood homes
> And moving, moving, on through scenes and towns
> Weep for the crowds, of men
> Like birds gone south forever. (22)

In these lines, the poet is beginning his explorations in the mythology of other cultures — in this case, essentially that of India — and is searching for ways to say what he so far has been unable to utter. Divesting himself as much as possible of the garb of Western poetic form, Snyder gropes his way toward the freedom of the void, the "place" beyond style and tradition where form and content are one. Stuttering like the idiot, or shaman, he attempts to "invent a tune, / . . . this moment one time true." Here Snyder's style is consistent with the visionary state of mind. The pure poetry Snyder seeks is beyond language and culture. It is experienced during inexpressible mystical states when one is transfixed, participating in a mutual energy flow. It is an act close to madness. In lines strikingly similar to those of Edgar Allan Poe, Snyder writes, "The long old chorus blowing underfoot / Makes high wild notes of mountains in the sea" (22).

"A Stone Garden" evidences Snyder's availability and watchfulness. Here is expressed his longing for the poem which springs up "full-armed." In section three, a new type of Snyder poem begins to emerge; for Snyder reaches beyond the strictures of the iamb, beyond the mental and stylistic limitations of a literary frame of reference. Associating the writing of a poem with dance and music, with inspiration beyond art and with the need to think and express oneself through language, Snyder attempts to leap form. Although he reaches ground already traversed by Pound and Williams ("a leap of words to things and there it stops."), Snyder offers the glimmer of territory yet untraveled: "And moving, moving, on through scenes and towns." The imagery is not contrived; it drifts up and out of Snyder's unconscious mind unassisted. The yearning to fill enclosures (caves, shops, domes) with sound — to give shape to unconscious forms, to bring them to the surface and articulate them — is evident. These lines are quite similar to Shamanistic poetry, the utterances of a primitive "medicine man" while in a trance state. They are "pure poetry," artificed only in the sense of being set down in words for presentation to the reader.

Like Robert Graves, whose important study of poetry and mythology, *The White Goddess*, influenced him,[14] Snyder has not been one to spurn the "Muse." As Snyder relates in *Conversations: Christian and Buddhist*, there is a type of poetry which goes beyond craft, beyond artifice, which Snyder calls the "stuttering voice of revelation."[15] This poetry emanates from another area of man's being outside his regular realm of experience; it is beyond personal control, training, and even self-knowledge. As Snyder relates, "My discipline as a poet, at least for the last decade, has been a discipline of openness and availableness."[16] Concerning that availability he states:

The problem is that you have to make the effort when it wants to spout forth. It's unpredictable, and it tends to speak at the most inconvenient times. . . . That's the discipline that I had to learn. Even to wake yourself up in the middle of the night and put it down. Of course it's learned, because you've applied yourself to all the poetry in the language and trained your ear to it. My friend the late Jack Spicer said, "All poetry is a mixture of static and the real thing." The static is your ego, talking, and the real thing is something else talking, and you can hardly tell which is which. But then you have to look at the poem with a ruthless eye. But for everyone I know who works in the realm of poetry, it makes you superstitious, and it makes you something of a gambler, because you can't count on ever writing another poem. You're not relying, in other words, on what you've accumulated in the way of wisdom or skill or reputation—you can only be an instrument of what comes.[17]

This is a more relaxed and spontaneous approach to poetry than that expressed in the poem "Riprap." At this level of creation, the act of writing poetry ceases to be work; it becomes creative response, rather than conscious effort. Poeticizing is no longer seen as an aggressive act of the ego. Clearly, at this pitch, Snyder is willing to sit and wait, attendant on the "Muse." Here is a different sense of craftsmanship. Craft functions, more properly, as deletion and revision; for the poet deletes what is not "real," he eliminates the chattering of the conscious mind. To Snyder, craftsmanship becomes knowing what to leave out. First practiced extensively in Snyder's second book, *Myths & Texts*, his use of the ellipse has aided the creation of a poem which comes increasingly closer to capturing in words the visionary state. This technique typifies what Snyder has called ". . . a totally new approach to the very idea of form."[18]

In subsequent works, after the beginnings made in *Riprap*, Snyder's movement away from established poetic forms becomes increasingly evident. In *Regarding Wave*, for example, where Snyder is at his best, he is frequently the instrument of the "Muse," the stuttering spokesman of revelation. The poet Robert Duncan quite correctly noted this aspect of Snyder's later work when he stated in an interview that Snyder is "not a maker."[19] Only after the poet has made himself available to that primitive state of mind does he act as maker. Since *Myths & Texts*, Snyder's conception of craft has changed and developed. At the risk of creating misunderstanding, but in the interest of clarification, it might be said that, in the later poems of Gary Snyder, poeticizing is regarded as more the act of a custodian than that of a carpenter. In "Some Yips & Barks in the Dark," written in 1966, Snyder makes this point specific:

For me every poem is unique. One can understand and appreciate the conditions which produce formal poetry as a part of man's experiment with civilization. The game of inventing an abstract structure and then finding things in experience which can be forced into it. A kind of intensity can indeed be produced this way — but it is the intensity of straining and sweating against self-imposed bonds. Better the perfect, easy discipline of the swallows dip and swoop, "without east or west."

Each poem grows from an energy-mind-field-dance, and has its own inner grain. To let it grow, to let it speak for itself, is a large part of the work of the poet.[20]

IV *"perfected attention"*

The poetic theoreticians of the first half of the twentieth century were concerned with bringing poetry into line with the discoveries of science, notably with empiricist psychology and physics. They demanded in poetry a reality consistent with that presented by science, and they attempted to develop objective criteria for creating and criticizing poetry. In short, poets and critics reacted against the prevalent Romanticism of nineteenth-century poetry. In the second half of the twentieth century, as Hyatt Waggoner has indicated,[21] contemporary poets — although they absorbed the pseudo-scientific notions of Pound and his followers and although they heeded their cry for objectivity — seem paradoxically to be reverting to selected Romantic notions. More and more American poets of the 1960's and 1970's — even poets such as Robert Lowell and John Berryman who learned their craft in universities dominated by the "New Criticism" — speak of the visionary, the passive, the nonstylistic aspects of poetry.

In his reverence for the imagination and in his distrust of ratiocination, Snyder also seems Romantic. In this respect, it might be suggested that Americans are hopelessly Romantic, even when they consider themselves to be hard-headed pragmatists. William Carlos Williams, for example, strove to hide his innate Romanticism after meeting Pound; and he was indignant when it was detected in his *Collected Poems* (1934) by Wallace Stevens, who wrote its Preface. Possibly such a response indicates that no one took the empiricist notions seriously, or that poets in general are incapable of objectivity. Certainly there is a relationship between poetry and science, and Snyder has alluded to the link; but art cannot be science, nor science art. And even science, as Alfred North Whitehead believes, is Romantic at the core.[22]

It would appear, then, that in the 1950's, 1960's and 1970's, the materialistic scientism of Imagism and the visionary aspects of Romanticism have coalesced. A spokesman for the new "controversy of poets," Robert Kelly writes, when attempting to explain this new poetic phenomenon, "what is at stake is a radical breakthrough in the nature of human consciousness and the nature of human verbal understanding."[23] Moving beyond the intellectual limitations of Imagism, yet maintaining the efficacy of its methodology, Kelly states, "The use of images constitutes a part of the poet's Vision. . . . Image is a vehicle for Vision."[24] Craft, therefore, becomes "perfected attention," states Kelly.[25] This view, of course, advocates a different sense of craft and form than that which passionately concerned poets in the early twentieth century. The terminology remains the same, but the meaning is different. Vision and craft (in the earlier senses of the terms) blend to create a new synthesis, one that is similar in many ways to Romanticism but that is essentially anti-Romantic.

Snyder's shift from artifice to vision might also be described in terms of Robert Bly's interest in association rather than in technique. Bly calls the visionary poem the "intense poem," and he states that "we get side-tracked into technique."[26] Bly points out that the poet should attempt to open ". . . new corridors into the psyche by association."[27] Thus, what is discussed here and evidenced in Snyder's poetry may actually not be a resurgence of

Romanticism or an unconscious rejection of the ideas of Pound and Williams. The new stress on vision, or the "true tradition of craft and form in our time,"[28] as Robert Kelly calls it, may more properly be seen as a development of the highly respected theories of the "masters" and as a movement from conception to perception as a more direct and "real" approach to poetry.

The similarity which Kelly sees in the work of Blake, Whitman, Pound, and Williams suggests this development. Pound is credited by most postwar poets with the first contemporary understanding of "Vision," and Williams is attributed with the theories of "freedom," "open form," and the transmission of Whitmanesque values and attitudes. According to Robert Creeley, "Pound . . . is back of all this, as is William Carlos Williams."[29] Certainly Pound's *The Cantos* and Williams' *Paterson* remain two of the most influential works of poetry. Charles Olson's method of "composition by field" and Denise Levertov's theory of "organic form" are developments based on the work of Williams and Pound.

The "truth" of modern poetry, as seen by Snyder and like-minded practitioners, is "revelation." Emanating directly from the natural world, these "ideas," as Williams called them, are contained in things themselves; and these ideas are liberated, not created, by the poet. T. S. Eliot and Stevens conceived of the poetic imagination as imposing form on the formless — of creating order out of disorder. More recent poets, however, tend to distrust created, or what is seen as artificial, order; instead, they seek a pre-existing, organic order. According to Hyatt Waggoner, the "new poet" believes he ". . . must lose his self-consciousness and immerse himself in 'process' in order to render a fragment of chaos 'concrete in a moment of time.'. . ."[30] In this light, Charles Olson considered poetry as an energy process. Action painting and the so-called musical "happening" of recent years indicate this change in the role of the artist. In this respect, the theories of contemporary poets, such as Snyder, seem distinctly non-Romantic in essence.

These poets have an entirely different perception of nature than that of the Romantics. Seeking a more personal relation to the universe, the Romantics asked many valid questions, but they were unable to decode the answers they received because of clinging Judeo-Christian bias; a humanistic view of the universe; and, most importantly, lack of scientific knowledge. In addition, they took their assumptions along with them, looking for "truth," "beauty," and "the eternal." Thus, before they started their journey they were hopelessly caught up in a linguistic relationship to the universe. Unlike Snyder and other contemporary poets, they thought in terms of mental constructs and not "things," to use Williams' terminology again. Ralph Waldo Emerson's transparent eyeball in actuality was nothing more than the decoder of a subjective "reality." Looking for Transcendental "sources," the Romantics were, in effect, only mythologizing the unconscious mind, a psychic process of which they knew little and thus considered as a "place." The Transcendentalists read the Orientals, and agreed, as does Snyder, that all was interrelated. Yet they stood aside, viewing what they called "Nature" as something other than themselves. The "answers" were coming from themselves, yet they saw them as external inspirations. In contrast to the perception of the world projected in Snyder's later work, the Romantics never *saw* nature. They were looking at their own minds.

CHAPTER 3

Loyalties

I "*il miglior fabbro*"

DURING college and the early years in San Francisco, Snyder's favorite poet was Ezra Pound according to Kerouac and other acquaintances. More recently, Snyder's debt to Pound has been mentioned by the poet-reviewer James Dickey and reiterated by many other critics. Snyder has indeed learned much from the old master; for similarities in technique, the cultural affinities, and even, if one looks closely at Snyder's biography, the striking comparison in life-style and approach to the writing of poetry are too obvious to be overlooked. Certainly, Pound's concern for *le mot juste* (the exact word) and for the simple, straightforward statement have become a part of Snyder's poetic canon. Pound's attention to the well-made line, the clean image, and his unflinching dedication to the unpropagandized perception are clearly evident in Snyder's work. One also sees concern for etched preciseness and truth even in the titles of these poets' work, Pound's *Section: Rock-Drill* and Snyder's *Riprap*, for example. Both titles relate rock and masonry to poems and to the act of writing poetry, and both indicate dedication to craft and love of tools and materials.

Urging rejection of *fin de siècle* wordiness and sentimentality, Pound, combining empiricist psychology with Oriental poetics, developed his theory of Imagism.[1] In his statement in 1912, Pound listed the principles of the esthetic which, although it did not found a lasting "school" of poetry, was to influence countless twentieth-century poets, Snyder among them. The principles were:

1. Direct treatment of the "thing," whether subjective or objective.
2. To use absolutely no word that does not contribute to the presentation.
3. As regarding rhythm: to compose in the sequence of the musical phrase, not in the sequence of the metronome.[2]

In these principles, as Pound later wrote in 1917, he attempted to create a poetry "harder and saner . . . nearer the bone." It would have "fewer painted adjectives," and it would be austere, direct, "free from emotional slither."[3] In short, Pound instructed poets to cut out the flab. He also stressed the use of the image, clearly and precisely rendered.

To Pound, the "image" was the basic unit of poetry. Paraphrasing the psychology of the day, Pound stated that the image was "that which presents an intellectual and emotional complex in an instant of time."[4] It would seem that Pound saw the poet as a scientist of sorts, for he was to collect the data of experience. According to Pound, the poem should present directly what is observed, the "thing," without interpretation or comment. This concern for representing the data of sense-experience in a sequence of images, skillfully, yet objectively, with as little intervention of the mind of the poet as possible, seems to have greatly impressed the young Snyder.

Although Snyder's early concern for craft, as well as tradition, has been discussed, another point in this regard in relationship to Pound's influence should be made. Early in his career, Snyder speculated about the possibility of writing a poetry which would capture nature truly. As he relates in his "Lookout's Journal," " — If one wished to write poetry of nature, where an audience? Must come from the very conflict of an attempt to articulate the vision 'poetry & nature in our time" (*Earth House Hold*, 4). This somewhat cryptic entry reflects Snyder's desire to get beyond the conventional romanticizing of nature, as Pound's Imagistic principles suggest; for too much nature writing was being done through rose-colored glasses. The experience observed and recorded is colored by the poet's biases and limitations. In addition, description of nature is often anthropomorphized: animals become "cute" and are often given human names, and mountains, rivers, and trees are "picturesque." Snyder, like Pound, sought the "real" in his "poetry of nature." And although Snyder knew that no description could be completely objective, and that what is "the real" is only the poet's own variation of it, he realized that poets *could* get closer to a realistic depiction or to a re-creation of nature than was thought possible. Pound paved the way.

Because of the tremendous explosion of knowledge in the late nineteenth century, a revolution in consciousness was affected. In response, twentieth-century poets strove to bring their level of awareness, and thus their art, into line with the "new sense of things" which science, psychology, and philosophy revealed. A ". . . revolution in man's experience of existence" occurred.[5] Taking its roots in the "objectivist" logic of Schopenhauer, transmitted through the work of Henri Bergson to T. E. Hulme, the British Imagist poet and philosopher, this new vision of experience prompted poets to attempt to experience what L. S. Dembo calls "essential reality"[6] by transcending the rational or conventional modes of apprehension, by rejecting the logical and the abstract, and by embracing the intuitive and concrete.

The "poets of reality," as they have been called by J. Hillis Miller, in their quest for realism, consequently rejected conceptualization; and, in response to the theories of Ludwig Wittgenstein, they even distrusted language which, according to one linguistic theory, makes conceptualization possible.[7] In short, conceptualization was regarded as idealistic — as the subjective creation of mental constructs *about* what is observed — rather than as the objective, direct, and sensuous apprehension of the universe as it is. Perception, therefore, becomes the accepted mode of "knowing" the objective world; for perception as a means to knowledge relates not to the *idea* of the thing but to the thing itself. William Carlos Williams, as indicated above, responded to this fact. As Miller has pointed out, the poet realized that, ". . . the mind must efface itself before reality . . . plunge into the density of an exterior world, dispersing itself in a milieu which exceeds it and which it has not made."[8]

Contemporary poets such as Charles Olson, Robert Bly, and Gary Snyder have expanded this realization. Realizing that there are no objects, no substance, only mutually interacting energy fields or, in human terms, experience, or process, these poets immerse themselves in experience, blending the so-called inner and outer worlds. In this regard, as critic John R. Carpenter was to write of Snyder's work, "It is the fidelity to a sense of the world which makes this poetry so valuable. It is profoundly unsolipsistic. The separation which we often allow to creep into our lives (inner world / outer world; rational / irrational; subjective / objective; ego / id) are absent."[9] Snyder's realism and eco-mysticism, blending "inner" and "outer" worlds, is evident in his objective rendering of detail.

For example, in "Water" from *Riprap* Snyder describes a typical wilderness experience with precision and objectivity:

Pressure of sun on the rockslide
Whirled me in dizzy hop-and-step descent,
Pool of pebbles buzzed in a Juniper shadow,
Tiny tongue of a this-year rattlesnake flicked,
I leaped, laughing for little boulder-color coil —
Pounded by heat raced down the slabs to the creek
Deep trembling under arching walls and stuck
Whole head and shoulder in the water:
Stretched full on cobble — ears roaring
Eyes open aching from the cold and faced a trout. (*Riprap*, 10)

In this poem, even though the poet is present as actor, observer, and reporter, the reader is not diverted from the essential experience of the wilderness. Although the poet obviously feels kindly toward the baby rattlesnake and the trout, he does not anthropomorphize them: they remain a snake and a trout. And, although Snyder's good feelings are contagious, he does not tell the reader how he should feel. The details are sparse, simple, and sensuous. Adjectives, as Pound prescribed, are few and spartan-like. The diction is verb- (*action* — Snyder descends to the stream) and noun- (*thing* — wilderness described) oriented. The dominant image centers are water, "tumbling, cold," and rock, "rockslide, slab, boulder." The metaphor, "pool of pebbles," links these image centers. The movement of the poem and the action it describes are fast-paced. The verbs, "whirled," "flicked," "leaped," "raced," "stuck," "stretched," and "faced" present a direct response to environment. This sequence of verbs, although grammatically past tense, presents the action as if it is occurring spontaneously before the reader's eyes. Man, trout, and the environment of which man is a part are brought into rapid conjunction. The reader's response, like the poet's, is surprise and delight.

By simply pointing to the "objects" in nature, Snyder removes himself to a great extent from the poem, but he blends himself, the action, and the scene. Thus he creates a more "real," or ecological picture, although he artistically renders these interrelated energy fields. In this poem, Snyder has come close to achieving Pound's early Imagistic goals. The "thing" is treated directly; no unneeded words are included. And the oral technique of using stress centers creates the rhythm and sets the pace of the poem. More importantly, through the use of linked images, Snyder has come close to recording nature as it is — not exactly as a scientist might, as Pound at first wished — but without undue comment or interpretation.

On another level, Pound has been both influence and model; for, as Richard Howard has pointed out, Snyder has "embraced and exalted"[10] the example of Pound. Although Howard was referring to Snyder's transformation of Pound's lyric measure, his statement may be interpreted in another sense. For Pound, in fact, was the exemplar of the poet as teacher and as culture-hero for many contemporary poets, and he was certainly that for Snyder. Through Pound's concern for the oral aspects of poetry, for the role of the poet as performer, and for his use of the reading as a didactic as well as a dramatic occasion, he influenced drastically the reading of poetry in America. In the figure of Ezra Pound, the public and private faces of the poet blend, coalescing in a mask of great power and attraction. Snyder's own readings, with their mixture of lyric and didactic elements, their musical chantlike quality, and their vivacity and spirit, are in these respects influenced by Pound.

Like Snyder, Pound did not neglect the social function of literature nor the role of poet as teacher and savior. *The Cantos,* which present Pound's personalized reading of history, were written to promote his view of Western culture's fall from greatness and to present the older values which he believed could sustain it. Cantos such as "Canto XLV," in which Pound states his cranky economic theories (on usury in this case), seem strikingly similar to some of the essays in Snyder's *Earth House Hold* in their didactic intent and in their cultural primitivism. Pound's alienation from American culture and his self-appointed mission as a hero influenced his ransacking of other cultures in search of basic principles and sounder values. His work, like Snyder's, is a synthesis of what he found. Neither poet feared to cross cultural barriers to select an example or to make a comparison. In this respect, Snyder has referred to Pound as "an American trying to construct a myth out of the *lore* of Europe and Asia with varying degrees of success."[11]

The striking similarities between Pound's *ABC of Reading* and Snyder's *Earth House Hold* point up the comparison between these poets' esthetic and cultural goals. Both books were written to teach: they are textbooks which, as Pound has written in his introduction to *ABC,* "can also be read 'for pleasure as well as profit' by those no longer in school; or by those who in their college days suffered those things which most of my own generation suffered."[12] Or, as Snyder states in his preface to *Earth House Hold,* his text is a collection of "Technical Notes & Queries To Fellow Dharma Revolutionaries." The didactic and revolutionary concerns of both these books are evident. As in *The Cantos* (especially 85–95), where Pound gives the meaning of history as he sees it in order to expose "the lies of history" and to hammer home the "truth" by reiteration, Snyder presents his view about poetry and history in *Earth House Hold*, and suggests the need for a revolution of consciousness. In short, in both these works the poets are creative heroes who are bravely working for the regeneration of Western culture.

The Orient, in particular, has been a source of inspiration and values for both poets. Although Pound never became interested in Buddhism because his personality drew him toward Confucius, and although Snyder's commitment to and knowledge of the cultures of India, China, and Japan is profound and Pound's attention casual, their mutual response to Chinese and Japanese poetry is worth mentioning. Describing the composition of his now famous Imagistic poem, "In a Station of the Metro," Pound explained how he rediscovered the *haiku*. This rediscovery of Oriental poetry and Pound's subsequent experimentations were to have great effect on modern poetry. Pound, however, unlike Snyder, who seems to have adapted the *haiku* form to his needs, never wrote a true *haiku;* in fact, he soon tired of the form. Pound's response to Oriental literature was essentially technical, and his understanding of its philosophical basis was superficial. Nonetheless, although Pound's early interest in Chinese and Japanese poetry seems to have shifted to scrutiny of ancient Chinese political, economic, and social theory (Cantos 52–61), he continued his not scrupulously literal translations from the Chinese, and, according to critics, captured admirably the spirit of the work translated.

Pound may not have been able to accept the philosophical basis of Oriental poetry — roughly speaking, the general assumption of the unity of all life forms — but he was thoroughly familiar with the technical aspects of the Imagistic Chinese and Japanese poems. Pound was aware that the central element of the classical Oriental poem is the image, the verbal structure which affects an instantaneous and profound insight. As Snyder has related in his journal, this is a poetry ". . . where the sound or sight HITS and is transformed by the mental . . . " (*Earth House Hold*, 41). Pound believed with Whitman that the British literary tradition was only one of many sources from which American poets could learn. His example helped to turn Snyder's eyes away from England and toward the Orient for modes of expression suited to presenting the new sense of things uncovered by modern science. In the present century, Pound broke this new ground first, if only in a cursory manner. In a very real way he helped to make Snyder's tilling of this Far Eastern soil possible.

II *"sharp blows on the mind"*

One of Snyder's earliest cross-cultural experiences, one which he remembers with great pleasure, concerns learning to use chopsticks in a Chinese restaurant in Portland, Oregon. Snyder's interest in matters Oriental, however, has been directed to more concerns than those of etiquette and his commitment was more than casual. Snyder has recently related that the influence of Medieval China on his mind was great. Geographically China was closer than Europe, as he relates, and looked like the Pacific Northwest.[13] After college, Snyder obtained an anthology of Oriental poetry, reading deeply and widely. In addition, Kenneth Rexroth's superb translations in *One Hundred Japanese Poems* impressed him. However, having read and studied Pound in college, Snyder most probably was first introduced to Oriental literature by the translation of *Nō* drama of Fenollosa made available by Pound in *Noh, or Accomplishment* (1916) and by Pound's own highly personalized translations of Chinese poetry.

Evidence of the impact of the Orient on Snyder is extensive. The structure of *Mountains and Rivers Without End* is based on Snyder's reading of *Nō* drama and is also patterned on the type of ancient Chinese scroll which unrolls horizontally and which gradually depicts the journey through mountains of a small Zen monk figure who is dwarfed by the rugged landscape. Snyder, who studied seriously both Chinese and Japanese, has translated numerous poems from both these languages. He has acknowledged his debt to the poets of T'ang China; and translator Wai-lim Yip in his introduction to *Hiding the Universe: Poems by Wang Wei* has recently stated that Snyder is the contemporary poet whose work most closely approximates in philosophy, tone, and style the Chinese poem of the T'ang dynasty poet-painter Wang Wei (701–760 A.D.).[14]

"Mid-August At Sourdough Mountain Lookout" offers a good example of the influence of Chinese poetry on Snyder's work:

> Down valley a smoke haze
> Three days heat, after five days rain
> Pitch glows on the fir-cones
> Across rocks and meadows
> Swarms of new flies.
>
> I cannot remember things I once read
> A few friends, but they are in cities.
> Drinking cold snow-water from a tin cup
> Looking down for miles
> Through high still air. (*Riprap*, 1)

Much could be written about the nature orientation, the quiet nostalgia, the peacefulness, and the satisfying solitude evident in this
poem, all of which are traits of the classical Chinese poem. What is
important in this context, however, is the impact upon the reader of
this poem of great immediacy which artistically captures, or re-
creates, a moment in time as if it is just occurring. There is no
forcing of the imagination. The images arrange themselves in lines
in the order of apprehension — the poet's and the reader's — thus,
the sense of spontaneity. The imagery is sensuous: the reader sees
the haze, feels the heat, and watches the pitch glow and the flies
swarm. The reader drinks cold water from a tin cup; and he muses,
as does the poet, while looking down through high, still air. As each
image is presented, the reader is hit by it and is transformed. The
experience then becomes his own. In addition, Snyder does not
moralize or offer commentary; he is describing the experience objectively. Yet, the reverberations — the associations and sugges-
tions which the poem creates — are profound. The reader continues the journey where the poem leaves off; and, completing the
experience, he gains a direct and deep perception of things.

This deceptively simple poem contains two stanzas and ten lines.
Much of the poem, possibly the core imagery and more, may have
been created in a flash. Like the Chinese poetry of the T'ang and
Sung Dynasties, this poem builds its effect through a sequence of
vivid natural images which produce strong responses in the reader's
mind. As Snyder writes, "In part the line was influenced by the five-
and seven-character line Chinese poems I'd been reading, which
work like sharp blows on the mind."[15] The second stanza offers, in
keeping with traditional Chinese nature poetry, the inevitable
human response to the description: "I cannot remember things I
once read / A few friends, but they are in cities." These two short

lines quickly and adeptly evoke the mood of solitariness with sad but somehow strangely pleasant melancholy.

Like the Zen-influenced Chinese nature poets, Snyder is removed from the crowd. Living ascetically in isolation, the poet loses touch with cities, with the crush of urban affairs, and even with his friends. The ambivalent, accepting quality of the poem is consistent with the Zen admonition to "drift like clouds and flow like water." The poem, although set in a Western American wilderness landscape, is grounded in an ancient esthetic tradition which Snyder has mastered and personalized. However, Snyder has also rearranged the traditional Chinese poetic structure. Instead of ending the poem with the poet's comments, as in most Chinese nature poetry, Snyder develops the imagery for three additional lines which extend the direction of the viewer's eyes and thus the range of the poem — out, away, and down from the mountain. The traditional poem would have either ended with the seventh line or would probably have included lines eight to ten in the poem after the fifth line.

Wu-ti, who lived in China over two thousand years ago, has written:

> The sound of her silk skirt has stopped.
> On the marble pavement dust grows.
> Her empty room is cold and still.
> Fallen leaves are piled against the doors.
> Longing for that lovely lady
> How can I bring my aching heart to rest?[16]

Although this poem, translated by Arthur Waley, is not written on the same subject and although the locale and mood are different, it is similar to Snyder's "Mid-August" in its essential aspects. Each line presents a distinct image that appeals to one of the senses, as does Snyder's — a "blow on the mind." Both poems were written in isolation and evoke a melancholy quality. And in Wu-ti's poem, there is also a sense of stillness, as if time had stopped, as if nature had frozen. In the Chinese poem, though, the four lines of natural imagery are culminated by the poet's statement of sentiment. With the word "rest," the poem is finished; the love affair is over; the woman, dead. Snyder's variation on this form, however, exhibits his mastery and versatility. By developing his poem three lines further, by rearranging the sequence of images, and by inserting his comment nearer to the middle of the poem, Snyder extends its range and emotional effect. As a result, the reader is able to feel the immensity of space and the great distances between human beings. Other poems in *Riprap*, such as "All Through the Rains," show this early and important poetic influence. Yet, continued use of this technique can be seen in the later collections, especially in *The Back Country*. In "Yase: September," which is especially distinctive, Snyder relates how old Mrs. Kawabata

> out of a mountain
> of grass and thistle
> she saved five dusty stalks
> > of ragged wild blue flower
> and put them in my kitchen
> > in a jar. (37)

The poignancy and extreme humanity of this act, presented in this image in typical Chinese style, strikes one deeply.

III   *"A far bell coming closer"*

While in graduate school, Snyder became interested in Buddhism. Later, he began to sit in meditation *(zazen)* and then to attend lectures at the First Zen Institute. Thus began his lifelong practice of Zen Buddhism, a most significant influence on Snyder as man and poet. In Jack Kerouac's *The Dharma Bums* (1958), the author gives a vivid sketch of Snyder and his interest in the Orient and Zen during these years. One detail stands out. In describing Snyder and his neat cottage in the Berkeley hills, Kerouac writes: "He had a slew of orange crates all filled with beautiful scholarly books, some of them in Oriental languages, all the great sutras, comments on sutras, the complete works of D. T. Suzuki and a fine quadruple-volume edition of Japanese haikus."[17] Amusing photographs of Snyder at this time, dressed in Japanese garb, can be found in the recent commemorative work for Kerouac, *Scenes Along the Road*. Upon first meeting Snyder, Ginsberg was to write in his journal, which is reproduced in this commemorative, "a bearded interesting Berkeley cat name of Snyder, . . . who is studying oriental and leaving in a few months . . . to be a Zen monk. . . ."[18]

Popular interest in Buddhism and the Orient in general flagged after the 1950's. But Snyder and the poet Philip Whalen, who had been Snyder's roommate at Reed College and is now a Zen priest, so deepened their practice that Buddhism became an integral part of their lives. As Snyder stated recently in an interview conducted while he was living in Kyoto, Japan, "So my spiritual career has been half in the realm of peyote and shamanism, American Indian contacts, nature mysticism, animism, longhair and beads, the other one-half concerned with the study of Sanskrit and Chinese and the traditional philosophies of the Orient."[19] For two decades Snyder has continued his translations, written reviews of Oriental works for scholarly journals, and extended his long discussion of Buddhism by composing poetic essays on its contribution to world thought.

The *bihhiku* (a wanderer, or man of the road), first presented to Americans in popular form in Kerouac's *The Dharma Bums*, seems to have been an early model for Snyder. A traditional Buddhist figure in the Orient, the *bihhiku* appears frequently in literature as a mendicant, dependent upon charity for subsistence. Snyder has made the connection between the American hobo, the romance of the road, and the *bihhiku*. By genteel standards the *bihhiku*, or Buddhist hobo, looks disreputable, paying little attention to his appearance. He holds himself above the affairs of the material world and is both a serious and comic figure; he acts in a way which often seems absurd; he frequently laughs at delicate moments, and yet by this action he vividly illustrates the ridiculousness of human vanity and acquisitiveness. The *bihhiku* is usually depicted in Chinese and Japanese ink paintings as round-bellied (indicating compassion), and as dressed in rags. In Western terms, he is the wise man as clown. Snyder depicts himself in serious-comic pose as *bihhiku* in the following poem which ends his "Lookout's Journal":

> "I am here to handle some of the preliminary
>   arrangements for the Apocalypse.
> Sand in pockets, Sand in hair,
> Cigarettes that fell in seawater
> Set out to dry in the sun.
> Swimming in out of the way places
> In very cold water, creek or surf
> Is a great pleasure."
> Under the Canary Island Pine
> zazen and eating lunch. We are all immortals
>   & the ground is damp. (*Earth House Hold*, 24)

In this poem, the poet, disheveled and grinning, is taking great pleasure in simply being alive. Nothing is complicated. Although the abstract idea of the coming "apocalypse" is stated and although the poet is seriously making the necessary arrangements to be prepared for it, he is also laughing at himself; he knows that an individual life means nothing in the scheme of things. The concrete details of the poem are what affect the reader most — the sand, the sea, the cigarettes, the lunch — for he is reassured by the truth of the final detail. That is, what is most important at this moment is the earth and the reader's relationship to it. As Snyder puts it, "the ground is damp." A typical Zen response, spontaneous and pragmatic, this comment presents the ideal of a voluntary, joyous poverty that is combined with direct attention to the details of physical life typical of the Zen Buddhist.

Alan Watts, in his now famous pamphlet *Beat Zen Square Zen and Zen,* reinforces this picture of Snyder as a holy bum and as a practitioner of what Watts calls "Zen" as opposed to "Beat," or "Square" Zen: "But Snyder is, in the best sense, a bum. His manner of life is a quietly individualist deviation from everything expected of a 'good consumer.' His temporary home is a little shack without utilities. . . . When he needs money he goes to sea, or works as a firewatcher or logger. Otherwise, he stays at home or goes mountain-climbing, most of the time writing, studying, or practicing Zen meditation."[20] As Watts indicates, Snyder maintains his interest in the *bihhiku* to this day, relating his respect for Padmasambhava, who brought Buddhism from India to Tibet, and for Hsuan-tsang, the central figure in "The Hump-Backed Flute Player" a section from *Mountains and Rivers Without End.*

Snyder's early distrust of Christianity may also have influenced him to look with favor on Buddhism. Snyder tells the story of how, although his parents were agnostic, they suggested that he sample local church services. At such a gathering he was told that animals did not have souls. After hearing this statement, Snyder relates, he knew that he had to look elsewhere for spiritual nourishment.[21] In "Toji" and "Higashi Hongwanji," published in *Riprap,* Snyder displays a religious response that is more akin to his own perception. Both poems describe temples in Kyoto, Japan; and what particularly interests Snyder, in contrast to his Christian experiences, is the complete lack of religiosity and sanctimoniousness in regard to these Oriental places of worship. When in church, a person must be quiet, wear certain clothes, and sit reverently; but in these temples, life is accepted in all its humanness, and ordinary actions occur and are not repressed. In "Higashi Hongwanji," Snyder relates, "In a quiet dusty corner" of the Shinshu temple are "Some farmers eating lunch on the steps" (19). In regard to the Shingon temple in "Toji," how unlike Western religious statues is the Buddha he sees: "A cynical curving round-belly" / . . . "Bisexual and tried it all . . . "(18). This Buddha is not ethereal and distant; he is extremely human and worldly. Snyder concludes, as if to make a final statement about Western religion, "Nobody bothers you in Toji . . . "(18).

In Japan, Snyder studied Zen Buddhism with Oda Sesso Roshi until his death in September, 1966. Sesso's teacher (*roshi*) had been Zuigan Gota; and Gota's had been Sokatsu Shaku; and Shaku's in turn had been the famous Abbot Soyen Shaku, the author of *Sermons of a Buddhist Abbot* (1906), a work of singular importance in the history of Buddhism in America. The transmission of Zen practice is direct through Sesso from Soyen to Snyder. Of Oda Sesso, Snyder writes that he was the "subtlest and most perceptive man I've ever met. He didn't display his power openly but appeared mild and silent."[22] Snyder dedicated *Earth House Hold* to Oda Sesso.

In Snyder's essay "Spring Sesshin at Shokoku-ji," first published in *Chicago Review* and later collected in *Earth House Hold*, Snyder describes the *roshi* and his application of Zen methodology. The *roshi* is responsible for the spiritual development of the community, and he accomplishes this awesome task partly through his brief, direct lecture-sermons called *teisho*, but primarily by directing his students in *sanzen*, the encounter between student and *roshi* in which the student is questioned and his progress toward enlightenment is uncovered. The student must demonstrate his progress, not simply verbalize it; for action, immediate and spontaneous, is most important in Zen. Snyder calls this encounter "the fierce face-to-face moment when you spit forth truth or perish — from him" (*Earth House Hold*, 45).

In *The Three Pillars of Zen*, Philip Kapleau writes of the *roshi's* behavior during *sanzen*: "Alternately he is the strict, reproving father who prods and chastens and the gentle, loving mother who comforts and encourages. . . . In a variety of ways the *roshi* will prod and nudge this mind into making its own ultimate leap to satori. . . . He shoots sharp questions at him, demanding instantaneous answers, or he jabs him suddenly with his baton, or slams at the mat or table, all in an effort to pry apart the student's delusive mind."[23] The actions of the *roshi* and Zen teaching seem, in general, strange and unnecessarily brutal, even cruel. But, since this study is not concerned with such behavior, the emphasis must be upon an examination of the basic Zen practice that provides a sufficient introduction to this important influence on the life and work of Gary Snyder.

The basic practice in Zen consists of *zazen* (sitting meditation), *koan* (philosophical question) study, and *sanzen* (interview with master). Orientals have understood the relationship between body and mind for thousands of years. Yoga is a discipline, or practice, with which most Americans are at least acquainted, which utilizes such an awareness. In short, the Orient has been aware that a person's psychology, or state of mind, depends greatly on the health of the body. Thus, in most Oriental body-mind disciplines, or practices, including Zen, or "sitting meditation," the practitioner must sit erect, back straight — spinal column taking the least tension — with legs crossed in what is called the "lotus" position. While sitting in this position for long periods, the student attempts to clear his mind and to remove the extraneous chatter of everyday life. Once he has learned to keep his mind still, the student is ready for *koan* study, which is administered by the *roshi* during *sanzen*.

Koans have become familiar to Western readers through the works of writers such as J. D. Salinger, and they are often used in literature to symbolize paradox. To the Western mind, *koans* seem like short, preposterous stories or, more specifically, the riddles that are impossible to solve. For example, the *koan* "What is the sound of one hand clapping?" is nonsensical since one hand cannot clap or produce a sound. Herein, however, lies the "method" — the word is important — behind such seeming inconsistency. Just as the Orient has been aware of the intimate connection between mind and body, psychology and physiology, it has also realized that logic — rational thinking — is inadequate as a basis for responding to complex, emotional experience. Man, who is more of an unconscious than a conscious being, lives on a much deeper level than most are aware. *Koan* study is a methodology through which the student is teased and frustrated into relinquishing his death hold on logic. The contradiction in the *koan*, of course, is logical, not existential; and Zen is grounded in a distrust of the conscious mind. Through repeated failure to "solve" the *koan*, the student gradually realizes that the *koan* cannot be "solved" logically. He learns to understand, to see in another way. Insights are gained intuitively and spontaneously, not through work, or conscious effort. This realization suggests a whole new kind of thinking, a different means of perception, a different level of consciousness. For most people, Zen suggests, life is not centered on reality but on an "idea" of reality. Men live in language and are trapped by it. Language and rationality, which, according to Zen Buddhists, is the workings of language in understanding mind, tell men only about their own minds. Zen addresses itself, therefore, to the nonverbal; and it stresses spontaneity and immediacy of response.

The philosophical and psychological influence of Zen Buddhism is clearly evident in the life and work of Gary Snyder. Although Snyder never became a *roshi* or took formal orders, as did poet and friend Philip Whalen, Snyder is a practicing Zen Buddhist. He lives simply; and, in typical Zen Buddhist style, he is a man of action who responds directly and forcefully to personal encounters. Neither optimistic nor pessimistic, he strikes the observer as frank, straightforward, and cheerful. Compassionate, but disciplined and not sentimental, he throws himself totally and without reservation into activities once he has made a decision.

As well as affecting Snyder's life-style and developing certain latent aspects of his personality, Zen most certainly has influenced his writing: it has provided inspiration and subject matter for a significant amount of his work. The *haiku*-like jottings in his journals, sections of *The Back Country*, his "poetic scroll" *Mountains and Rivers Without End*, his Zen translations, and his later essays indicate this Zen influence. Poems from *Riprap*, such as "Kyoto: March" and "A Stone Garden," take their inspiration and setting from his first years as a Zen student in Japan. In "A Stone Garden" in *Riprap* (21), Snyder relates how he "prowled Tokyo like a bear / Tracking the human future / Of intelligence and despair." In "Six Years" in *The Back Country* (51–63), Snyder poetically captures the Zen experience related in his essay, "Spring Sesshin at Shokoku-ji." In the section entitled, "December," he describes his practice and alludes to his approaching enlightenment or, in Zen terms, *satori:*

> Sit until midnight. Chant.
>> Make three bows and pull the futon down.
>> roll in the bed —
>> black.
>
> A far bell coming closer. (*The Back Country*, 63)

"Journeys," the last section of *Mountains and Rivers Without End*, concludes with a section reminiscent of a Zen tale. Like a *koan*, it relates paradoxically that one must die in order to attain the enlightenment represented as the back country. It is an anecdote which displays the incomprehensible and illogical behavior of Zen adherents. Although this section is discussed later in detail in another context, two points in regard to its relationship to Zen and Snyder should be brought out at this time. The poet and Ko-san, described in the poem, stand on a cliff looking into a rock-walled canyon. When the poet asks what lies ahead, Ko answers, "That's the world after death." The poet thinks it looks no different from the territory they have been traveling. Ko grabs the poet and pulls him over the cliff.

The reader might draw from this anecdote that life and death are mutually interrelated, that they are merely extensions of each other, or different levels of consciousness. Also, to reach the "back country," the place of total freedom, man must die. Of course, this concept seems preposterous; for to die is to be nonexistent. Logically, no one goes anywhere after death. But in Zen terms, man must, in a sense, surrender life — must lose his ego and become selfless to find freedom. Only action, being pulled off a cliff, or in Zen terms being pushed over the edge of self, or driven out of the mind, can affect this liberation. Much as the student is prodded in formal Zen practice, the poet is prevented from asking further questions and from theorizing about the answers given: ". . . what's that up there. . . ." "I thought it looked / just like the land we'd been travelling, and couldn't / see why we should have to die" (*Mountains & Rivers Without End*, 42). In short, this passage from "Journeys" dramatizes the essential dilemma of mind-oriented man as understood by classical Zen and presented by Snyder. Only spontaneous action, like the slap of the Zen master, or the pull of Ko-san will produce results.

Many references to Zen appear in Snyder's early journals. Snyder's Zen admonitions to himself are swift, austere, and, at times, humorous. For example, ". . . there is more than enough time for all things to happen: swallowing its own tail" (*Earth House Hold*, 11); and "Don't be a mountainer, be a mountain. / And shrug off a few with avalanches" (*Earth House Hold*, 21). Other Zen-like statements are scattered throughout the journals; and they are terse, gem-like bits of doctrine tempered by the solitary lookout's wilderness experiences. For example,

> the boulder in the creek never moves
> the water is always falling
> together! (*Earth House Hold*, 2)

As is necessary in the practice of Zen, Snyder is relaxed; he is accepting and attentive to the life around him; but he is distrustful about thought and formal learning. The Zen insight of this statement gives the reader a sense of living nature, of process at work.

Growing Zen sensibility, similar to that evident above, is apparent in

> Are other worlds watching us?
> The rock alive, not barren
>   flowers lichen pinus albicaulis chipmunks
> mice   even grass. (*Earth House Hold*, 6)

Snyder's musing relates directly to the Four Vows of Zen. The first vow states, "Sentient beings are countless. I vow to save them all." In this statement, the reader can see an awareness that everything, in a sense, is alive. There is a strong nonhumanistic bias to Zen, and Snyder displays it in these lines. The sacramental view is presented that all is holy, even grass and chipmunks. More than fifteen years later, Snyder was to write a similar passage in his long, eco-religious poem, "Smokey the Bear Sutra," which was modeled after classical Buddhist religious texts:

> Once in the Jurassic, about 150 million years ago,
> The Great Sun Buddha in this corner of the Infinite
> Void gave a great Discourse to all the assembled elements
> and energies: to the standing beings, the walking beings,
> the flying beings, and the sitting beings — even grasses,
> to the number of thirteen billion, each one born from a
> seed, were assembled there: a Discourse concerning
> Enlightenment on the planet Earth.

In the line, "Each one born from a seed," Snyder implies that there is spirituality in everything, even in the lowly grasses.

Zen, as suggested above, is in many ways ecological in outlook and orientation. The central concept of ecology is internal relationship: all forms of life are interrelated, dependent in some way on other components of a vast "web of life." As Snyder has written in his journals, " '. . . there are no calendars in the mountains' — shifting of light & cloud, perfection of chaos, magnificent *jiji mu-ge* / interlacing interaction" (*Earth House Hold*, 15–16). He also writes, "Nature a vast set of conventions, totally arbitrary, patterns and stresses that come into being each instant; could disappear totally anytime; and continues only as a form of play: the cosmic / comic delight" (*Earth House Hold*, 21). There is also an evolutionary aspect to Zen, for life forms develop into other life forms. As Snyder points out in "Four Changes" — his ecological broadside which is grounded in Zen Buddhism as well as in scientific knowledge — all life is change; and men must accept this fact: "Everything that lives eats food, and is food in turn." This cyclic, ecological sense of nature is again referred to in the journals when Snyder asks,

> What happens all winter; the wind driving snow; clouds —
> wind, and mountains — repeating
>
> this is what always happens here. . . . (*Earth House Hold*, 7)

In another entry, Snyder plays with a line from the Buddhist sutra *"Prajna-paramita"* which is chanted in Zen monasteries. In "Crater-*Shan*" (using the Chinese "shan" for mountain), August 3, 1952, Snyder writes: "How pleasant to squat in the sun, / Jockstrap & zoris" (*Earth House Hold*, 5). This statement is followed by the statement that "form — leaving things out at the right spot / ellipse, is emptiness"(5). Although cited separately, these two statements go together as if one poem. The reader may notice at once the concreteness and simplicity of this *haiku*-like poem in contrast to the profundity of the thought it expresses. The poet is sparsely dressed; he is "leaving things out . . ."; but, more importantly, Snyder has applied the Buddhist doctrine of the sutra ("Form is emptiness, emptiness is form") to poetry. Developing his literary aesthetic, he concludes that the best form is organic. As Pound teaches and Snyder's Buddhism indicates, the poet must leave things out of his statements. Technically, this practice implies the use of the ellipse; and this specific application of Zen teaching to writing impresses the reader and the critic with the realization that Zen has had a deeper and more significant effect on the poetry of Gary Snyder than might be thought. Snyder's response to Zen is not simply cultural; the influence of Zen Buddhism clearly operates in Snyder on the psychic and esthetic level by actually shaping the creative act.

IV   *"reverberations"*

Undoubtedly, Snyder's study of Buddhism introduced him to the Zen-influenced poetic form, the *haiku*. After college, obviously fascinated with the form — its freedom, vividness, spontaneity, and close attention to nature — Snyder wrote many *haiku* poems such as those cited below that are taken from his journals at that time.

This morning:

floating face down in the water bucket
a drowned mouse. (*Earth House Hold,* 4)

two butterflies
a chilly clump of mountain
flowers. (*Earth House Hold,* 7)

Like Matsuo Bashō, the classic Zen poet of seventeenth-century Japan, Snyder has used the *haiku* extensively. The *haiku* is found in his short poetic essays, in larger poems as interludes, and in the travel journals, such as those found in *Earth House Hold*. The poet Allen Ginsberg has stated that Snyder is one of the few American poets capable of writing genuine *haiku*.[24] And Thomas Lyon has even gone so far as to state that the *haiku* is "the guiding principle of Snyder's poetics, whatever the length of the application."[25]

Haiku, or *hokku* as it was called in seventeenth-century Japan, is the shortest of the traditional Japanese poetic forms. It is a poem of seventeen syllables, divided into three lines. Matsu Basho (1644–94), one of the poets responsible for this development, accepted the Buddhist's first premise that all life is impermanent. Thus, he called for a poetry of mood and suggestion, rather than of intellect and statement. He insisted on five qualities: inspiration, fragrance, reverberation, reflection, and lightness. To this influential practitioner, *haiku* had to be a spontaneous expression of insight, grounded in an awareness of mortality. Yet it had to be light, effortless, compact, and profound; to be haunting in its implications; and to produce an effect similar to that which occurs when a stone is thrown into a clear pool of water — that is, rings in rings, or what Bashō calls "reverberations." Traditionally, the *haiku* must be concerned with nature and evoke a sense of one of the four seasons.[26] On a deeper level, *haiku* should develop one of the four basic Zen moods, or *furyu: sabi* (solitary and quiet), *wabi* (depressed or empty), *aware* (intense, nostalgic sadness connected with autumn), and *yugen* (the perception of something mysterious and strange).

The method of writing *haiku* is quite interesting. In that Japanese, like Chinese, is a language written in characters (ink brush-stroke pictures on rice paper), the early *haiku* were as much like paintings as they were poems. The reader not only read *haiku* for its semantic sense, or linguistic "meaning," but also the pictorial representation of the emotion which the poem presented. In short, *haiku* was a work of art in two senses, on two levels, or in two mediums. Although grammaticaly incorrect, *haiku* might be called a work of arts. In addition to the visual element in *haiku* is the strong Zen influence of spontaneity mentioned above, especially in relation to the creative act. Zen insists upon spontaneity and upon the acceptance of the consequences of actions. As applied to the writing of *haiku* with brush and ink on rice paper, this admonition produces interesting results. When inspired, the poet strokes the paper with the brush and does not pause until the poem is finished. Afterwards, no corrections or revisions are or can be made. Like the Zen life of egolessness through discipline, the writing of *haiku* is, in a sense, an artless but visionary experience. The poet abandons himself to the experience and simply responds to its call. Of course, it must be added, as in Zen, the best poets were those who had mastered all the brush strokes first and who had then gone beyond that discipline to complete freedom. The discipline and the mastery of the tradition came first. Through such mastery, spontaneity and freedom developed.

Often, *haiga* and *zenga*, informal paintings by Zen monks, accompanied *haiku* and were also influential in its development. The most common of these paintings were circles, bamboo branches, birds, or human figures drawn with powerful strokes; and the paintings of Sesshu (1421–1506) are a good example. *Zenga* and *haiga* represent the most extreme form of *sumi* painting, according to Orientalist Alan Watts; they are the most "spontaneous, artless, and rough, replete with all those 'controlled accidents' of the brush in which the exemplify the marvelous meaninglessness of nature itself."[27] Snyder, describing his early Zen activities while a fire lookout, relates that he "First wrote a haiku and painted a haiga for it; then repaired the Om Mani Padme Hum prayer flag, then constructed a stone platform, then shaved down a shake and painted a zenga on it, then studied the lesson" (*Earth House Hold*, 8). Directly following this notation in the journal is the following *haiku:*

> a butterfly
> scared up from its flower
> caught by the wind and swept over the cliffs
> SCREE (8)

Although this poem is very much like the traditional *haiku*, the reader notices Snyder's variation on the form: he has added a fourth line, and he has utilized a geological term in an interestingly new sense. "Scree" is rock which slides off mountains. In the poem Snyder has employed its meaning metaphorically by suggesting that the butterfly is like a falling rock. He has also utilized the sense of the sound of the term, for to say "scree" is to sound like one is screaming.

Haiku, like Zen responses to questions, are abrupt and direct; they are stated without thought, certainly without rumination. As does Zen, *haiku* tries to capture a "live moment in its pure 'suchness'."[28] To do so, it makes profound use of silence, or technically of ambiguity and implication; it says little but produces great effect. In a sense, *haiku* is almost wordless poetry. It is a poetry in which the reader is invited to participate and must do so. As Bashō has written, the *haiku* should exhibit and affect a child's sense of wonder and astonishment; this quality of sparseness and wonderment is present in Snyder's

> leaning in the doorway whistling
> a chipmunk popped out
> listening (*Earth House Hold*, 7)

As this poem indicates, *haiku* uses the simplest language, and it avoids academic, literary, or technical terms. In this respect,

Snyder writes in his journal, "One does not need universities and libraries / one need be alive to what is about" (*Earth House Hold*, 2). Thus, *haiku* is more human, more directed toward common experience. Although a Chinese of the T'ang Dynasty, writing poems more similar to *waka*, Han-shan's *Cold Mountain Poems* evoke this sense of the ordinary found in *haiku*. A typical Zen hermit, living alone in the mountains, unconcerned about dress, food, and lodging, Han-shan (627–50 A.D.) wrote poems spontaneously on trees, bark chips, and cave walls. Snyder has translated some of them, such as number 11:

> Spring-water in the green creek is clear
> Moonlight on Cold Mountain is white
> Silent knowledge — the spirit is enlightened of itself
> Contemplate the void: this world exceeds stillness. (*Riprap*, 47)

As in the following poem, the influence of Snyder's writing of *haiku* is evident. In Poem 19, Snyder translates:

> Once at Cold Mountain, troubles cease —
> No more tangled, hung-up mind.
> I idly scribble poems on the rock cliff,
> Taking whatever comes, like a drifting boat. (*Riprap*, 55)

Both in spirit and imagery this translation approximates *haiku*. The last line is particularly interesting in this respect, for the poet will accept life as it is and drift like a boat.

Clearly, Snyder did not apply the *haiku* as Bashō intended; for, as with other literary influences, he makes creative and individualized adaptations. One major reason for this liberty was Snyder's intention to capture the particular quality, or "suchness," of the wilderness experience, one unknown to the Medieval Japanese. In the following *haiku*, Snyder, the lookout, is at ease; he is viewing the mountain and making observations of a concrete and specific nature:

> on the west slopes creek beds are brushy
> north-faces of ridges, steep and
> > covered late with snow (*Earth House Hold*, 8)

> sitting in the sun in the doorway
> picking my teeth with a broomstraw
> listenin[g] to the buzz of the flies. (*Ibid.*, 8)

In these poems, little escapes Snyder; his scrutiny of and his commitment to the natural environment are complete. But the Japanese
sense of nostalgia is absent; and, strictly speaking, the poet captures
none of the Zen moods, unless it is *sabi* (solitary and quiet).
Nonetheless, Snyder's adaptation of the form works for him, for he
adequately re-creates and communicates quickly and simply this
moment of wilderness timelessness.

Additional evidence of Snyder's use of the *haiku* is found in *The
Back Country*. Many are excellent adaptations of the form, such as
those found in "The Public Bath":

> the baby boy
>> on his back, dashed with scalding water
>> silent, moving eyes
>> inscrutably
>> pees. (41)

Or in "Eight Sandbars on the Takano River":

> *strawberrytime*
>> walking the tight-rope
>> high over the streets
>> with a hoe and two buckets
>>> of manure. (44–45)

At times, however, Snyder's use of the *haiku* form is conscious and
seems somewhat contrived. This effect very often occurs when
Snyder uses the form to describe subjects other than nature. For
example, in his highly structured poem "Hitch Haiku," he relates
the events of a journey by linking descriptive *haiku:*

> They didn't hire him
>> so he ate his lunch alone;
> the noon whistle
>
> . . .
>
> Cats shut down
>> deer thread through
> men all eating lunch. (28)

Some of the *haiku* in this poem are less effective than they might be
because an inherent literary quality, reminiscent of Homer, seems to

remove the poem from experience. For example, "Sunday dinner in Ithaca — / the twang of a bowstring." (30) And the following poem, full of concrete, commonplace details, reminds the reader in this respect of William Carlos Williams' poem about the red wheelbarrow:

> Drinking hot sake
> toasting fish on coals
> the motorcycle
> out   parked in the rain. (31)

Nonetheless, there are *haiku* in "Hitch Haiku" which measure up to those cited earlier and, in fact, are not strictly speaking about nature. They exhibit Snyder's Zen wit and wonderment at its best.

> *Over the Mindanao Deep*
>
> Scrap brass
> dumpt off the fantail
> falling six miles. (29)

And the delightful *haiku:*

> After weeks of watching the roof leak
> I fixed it tonight
> by moving a single board. (30)

Clearly, *haiku* was a convenient poetic form for the young and developing poet Snyder; it blended his interests in Zen and the Orient. It suggested and re-created a response to a life of freedom beyond discipline which he was working toward in his personal life. It exhibited a strong resemblance to Imagistic theory and practice which fascinated him at this time. And it was a form which was easily adapted to his need to capture wild nature and the life of the common man.

V   *"all roads descend toward town"*

One other connection between Snyder and Zen, that of Oriental art, remains to be considered. The influence of Zen and Oriental art combine to produce many of his poems. In this respect, Snyder has

been significantly influenced by the Zen scroll. This scroll-like quality of Snyder's work is evident in poems such as, "Work To Do
Toward Town":

> Venus glows in the east,
>   mars hangs in the twins.
> Front on the logs and bare ground
>   free of house or tree.
> Kites come down from the mountains
> And glide quavering over the rooftops;
>   frost melts in the sun.
> A low haze hangs on the houses
>   — firewood smoke and mist —
> Slanting far to the Kamo river
>   and the distant Uji hills.
> Farmwomen lead down carts
>   loaded with long white radish;
> I pack my bike with books—
>   all roads descend toward town. (*The Back Country*,
> 49)

The vertical nature of this poem is obvious because of its contrast to
the horizontal movement achieved essentially through narration in
most poems. In this poem, although the poet is preparing for a
journey, he has not as yet left. The movement of his gaze goes from
the planets to the mountains, down over the houses, to the river
slanting far away to the distant hills, and then, with the mention of
the farmwomen going to market as he packs his bike with books,
moves on and down the hill to town. This adept, vertical movement,
creates a sense of distance very much capturing the visual propor-
tions and lengthened effect of the classical Chinese scroll.

There is a great sense of depth, as if the viewer could look out a
thousand miles; and this feeling captures the quality of a classical
mountain landscape in which there is no horizon and in which space
is boundless. Usually the bottoms of these paintings contain some
natural or domestic scene which captures and holds the viewer's
eye, but the tops are undefined. The eye is given nothing to focus on
and thus continues out into space. Similarly, this poem has only one
stanza, with no sections, only a steady, flowing movement. It is as if
Snyder directs the reader's eyes to the top of a scroll, a living
painting in which he and the farmwomen are the small human
figures going about their affairs, and then leads them downward. He

begins in space, "Venus glows in the east, / mars hangs in the twins." Then he focuses on the mountains; then back to the mountain village, and finally, in the reader's minds, down to the town.

Clearly, something quite interesting has happened here. Whereas, the eye usually moves from the bottom to the top of a scroll, that is from the substantial (vegetation, habitation) to the less substantial (past the mountain peaks and pines to the sky), Snyder has reversed this process in his poem. The poem is more concerned with man and his affairs, with the significance and importance of his life; and readers, who are made more aware of this fact, come away from the poem with a greater sense of the human situation. Readers are made aware that beyond them is nothingness — Venus, Mars, the stars and then what? The fact that no one knows is Zen awareness. Although men see mountains, birds, and the village in the poem, they are most interested in the farmwomen with their loads of "long white radish" and the poet and his books. Certainly humans find other humans most interesting. And Snyder, adapting a technique of Oriental painting to his own needs, enlivens this fact.

The reader cannot help but note the insubstantial, other-world quality of the first three-fourths of the poem; for everything seems to float, to drift, as in the works of the ancient Oriental painters. Snyder has used the lightest brush strokes to capture temporal life suspended in the void. As in the scrolls, a few jagged lines become a mountain; a "W"-line represents a bird; a circular stroke, an old hunched villager; and the absence of strokes, space and distance. To accomplish the effect Snyder has used verbs and adverbs to good effect, in addition to the details he has chosen to relate, most of which are insubstantial and transient. Although active in voice, these verbs are nearly passive in effect. To hang from something is to commit an action, but this action is what many would, in its effect, call passive. Frost is free of houses or melts in the sun. But again, these actions are the result of forces working on something. Thus, in effect, what is stated grammatically as active is, in actuality, passive. What is stated as action in the first degree (self-initiated) is actually response (reaction), or action in the second degree. This meditative, tranquil, remote quality, this inactive, passive stance, is evident in the poem and well developed.

Clearly, Snyder has adapted techniques from Oriental painting to his own needs. He has, like the painter, played with his reader's eyes and taken him on a journey. He has created a sense of insubstantiality like the nothingness of the universe, and then focused attention on the tiny figure of man who is relatively insignificant in the scheme of things but who is, nonetheless, important in his own way. After the floating quality of the first three-fourths of the poem, readers are glad to center in on man. The Williamsesque farmwomen and their now very significant "long white radish" take on greater meaning after the long journey from the planets and stars to the little mountain village suspended above the Kamo River and the valley. Even the poet himself finally draws the reader's attention: he carries those mysterious books. How interesting man is!

One of the aspects of Oriental landscape painting that has always impressed the viewer is the small proportion of the whole surface of the landscape which the little figure of the traveler or worker occupies. Yet, it is inevitable that the viewer's eyes dwell on him once they have returned from their initial trip to the top of the scroll. This response is a simple matter of visual perception; but on another level, it occurs simply because man prefers to understand things in terms of himself. He needs something concrete like white radishes and books to cling to. In this respect, in an unusually humanistic statement, Snyder has written, "I will not cry Inhuman & think that makes us small and / nature great, we are, enough, and as we are . . ." (*Riprap*, 27).

CHAPTER 4

Creating a Myth

ALTHOUGH published after *Riprap*, *Myths & Texts* was
Snyder's first completed work.[1] The title, taken from the anthropologist John R. Swanton's "Tlingit Myths and Texts,"[2] is cited
in Snyder's bachelor's thesis which was written in 1950–51 at Reed
College and in which many of the basic themes of *Myths & Texts*
were first traced. *Myths & Texts* is not a group of casual poems
collected under an interesting title; it is an imaginative application
of anthropological materials. In Snyder's explanation of the creation
of *Myths & Texts*, he states that the book "grew between 1952 and
1956. Its several rhythms are based on long days of quiet in lookout
cabins; setting chokers for the Warm Springs Lumber Company
(looping cables on logs and hooking them to D8 Caterpillars —
dragging and rumbling through the brush); and the songs and
dances of Great Basin Indian tribes I used to hang around."[3]

More specifically, the title, as Snyder writes, "also means the two
sources of human knowledge — symbols and sense-impressions."[4]
To Snyder, "myths" are the constructs through which men perceive
and understand the "texts," the physical world, or what they call
reality. Thus, "myths" relates to men's conceptions; and "texts," to
their physical environment. In *Myths & Texts*, Snyder moves from
past to present, from nature experienced to history imagined, from
the personal to the universal, and from the textural to the mythic.[5]
The locales of the various poems shift from the American Northwest
to the Orient. And into the narrative element is woven a great deal
of quotation that is often esoteric, in the Pound manner.

The central themes of *Myths & Texts* are the result of Snyder's
studies at Reed College and his observations of and meditations
upon the relationship between man and nature. Snyder's first work
on these themes is found in his thesis which has the following
characteristics: clarity and precision, innate poetic quality, and
cross-cultural bias. Although poets usually stress the negative

influence of college and university study on their work, (for example, Thoreau, although Henry Seidel Canby has proved otherwise)[6], evidence exists which indicates that the reverse is also true and that it was the case with Snyder. The Reed College experience (1947–51) undoubtedly had a significant influence; for Snyder's thesis is surprisingly good, thorough, and forcefully written. It evidences his potential as scholar but, in addition, shows his deeper inclination toward poetry. At Reed, Snyder took the opportunity to use his imagination as well as the academic analytical abilities which he was taught to develop. Clearly, formal education had an important effect on the mind of Gary Snyder and is evident in *Myths & Texts*. Although the poems are grounded in actual experience, *Myths & Texts* is a scholarly and, in a certain sense, academic work. The idea for these poems was probably conceived before his lookout and trail crew experiences (1952–54), and *Myths & Texts* bears the clear impression of Snyder's studies at Reed College, as well as the imprint of his extracurricular interests. As stated above, even the title of the work is adapted from a scholarly article.

However, *Myths & Texts* evidences many influences. Before discussing in sections III, IV, and V of this chapter the three central metaphors which unify *Myths & Texts* ("logging," "hunting," and "burning"), a consideration of three important influences will be undertaken. First, and most obvious, as critics have pointed out, is the influence of Ezra Pound. Pound's use of the ellipse, his juxtapositioning of quotations, his loose thematic linking of sections, and his use of exoteric, non-Western materials is evident. Since Pound's influence has already been discussed in detail in Chapter three, further discussion seems unnecessary. Second, in the conception of the work, Snyder seems to have been significantly influenced by the theories or, more specifically, by the admonitions of psychologist Carl Gustav Jung, as interpreted by Joseph Campbell. And third, if less obvious, is the example offered Snyder by the work of T. S. Eliot. In many respects, *Myths & Texts* is strikingly similar to Eliot's "The Waste Land," one of the basic models for contemporary mythic literature.

I *"A hero ventures forth"*

Developing and extending Freud's theory of the "subconcious mind," Carl Jung believed that a level of universal knowledge existed in the mind. He considered the "unconscious," as it later became known, to be a storehouse of images based not only on formative experiences but also on the basic experience of all humanity. These images were a kind of inborn *homo sapiens* knowledge, or common experience, and this area of human experience, which he called the "collective unconscious," was evident in myth. To Jung, the myth was the fundamental dramatic representation of man's deepest instinctual life, or what Snyder, in discussing Jung in his thesis, calls a re-arising of primordial reality in narrative form. Myths, therefore, are descriptions of man's innermost needs; and as Snyder states, "Reality is a myth lived . . . it provides a symbolic representation of projected values and empirical knowledge within a framework of belief which relates individual, group, and physical environment, to the end of integration and survival."[7]

Deeply aware of the psychological and cultural functions of literature, Snyder, like Jung before him, became deeply interested in how literature as myth effects consciousness — the structure, alteration, and fulfillment of psychological needs. In this respect, Jung, in *Psychology of the Unconscious*, suggests that it might be possible to create literature from the symbols in Frazier's *Golden Bough* which, in Snyder's words, ". . . would function in modern civilization — for individuals — as myth functions in primitive culture for the group. In doing so, the poet would not only be creating workable private mythologies for his readers, but moving forward the formation of a new social mythology."[8] What interests Snyder, then, is the psychological process of myth formation and man's consequent symbolic behavior or, in short, the way in which myth "dovetails with basic mental processes."[9] Under the influence of his readings in the works of Jung and Joseph Campbell, Snyder became deeply interested at the beginning of his career in myth and was charged by its social possibilities. Attempting objectives similar to those of Thoreau and Pound, Snyder began mythologizing his own life experiences; he became in effect Campbell's "creative hero" who was seeking personal liberation, the formation of a new social mythology, and, ultimately, the regeneration of society.

In *The Hero With a Thousand Faces*, Joseph Campbell, a significant exponent of the theories of Jung, develops the thesis that the quest motif is the key to all effective mythology. In Snyder's words, this central motif, or "monomyth," the basis of all mythology, ". . . corresponds on the one hand to primitive rites of initiation, and on the other to the psychological journey into the unconscious required of the individual who would attain 'wholeness'. . . ."[10] According to Campbell, this archetypal journey occurs in three stages — separation, initiation, and return: "A hero ventures forth from the world of common day into a region of supernatural wonder: fabulous forces are there encountered and a decisive victory is won: the hero comes back from this mysterious adventure with the power to bestow boons on his fellow man.[11] As Campbell further describes this experience, "The passage of the mythological hero may be overground incidently: fundamentally it is inward — into depths 'where obscure resistances are overcome, and long lost, forgotten powers are revivified, to be available for the transfiguration of the world.' "[12]

Snyder's adaptation of Campbell's "monomythic" structure is sketchy, and it does not order the poem. There is little linear movement in *Myths & Texts*. However, what most evidently is the unifying force of the poem is the poet as "creative hero" — his personality, wit and wisdom. A quick summary of the little "action" in *Myths & Texts* in terms of Campbell's monomyth may clarify this point. In *Myths & Texts*, when the "creative hero" travels through the back country of Western America in a search for new myths, he separates himself from others: he is initiated; and he returns with the "boon," in this case love and acceptance of humanity and man's state in nature. "Logging" presents the state of affairs more specifically. This first section sets the stage, so to speak, for "Hunting"; and this first step in the quest, as outlined by Campbell, is separation. When the poet sits alone beside the road "without thoughts . . . Hatching a new myth . . ." ("Hunting, 1"), the quest for wisdom has begun. In this second section of the poem, the poet introduces his teachers, the animals and other lower forms of life, and the Indians (his human teachers). The reader hears their songs and lives in and through their myth. In addition, the poet as "creative hero" explores realms strange to ordinary man. Although his trip is represented in terms of physical, wilderness territory, it is basically psychic. On this journey, the poet learns archaic ways, and is, in short, re-educated — he is *re*-taught, *un*learned, and *de*-civilized. In this respect, in "Hunting" the reader learns that all beasts are alive and have a kind of a soul. Here, there is also the suggestion of the trials to come, of the tests which the "creative hero" must pass in the next and final section.

The second shaman's song heralds the second stage of the journey of the "creative hero" — the initiation. The poet makes what Snyder has called ". . . preliminary arrangements for the apocalypse . . ." (*Earth House Hold*, 24). According to Hindu mythology which informs this section, in this *yuga (Kali)*, or geological and historical time period, all will end in fire. Then a "golden age" will again occur. Accordingly, in the poem, the "River recedes," and the sun dries the shaman as he dances. The final test approaches. In the poems which follow this introduction, the hero relates his awareness of the existential nature of existence, and tells how he saw "hell" — how he suffered in his quest for wisdom. The poet speaks of "terrible meditations" in "Burning, 12," and he describes his mythic journey into the unconscious in "Burning, 3." In "Burning, 14," the "creative hero" returns to society; and this is the third stage. Snyder writes, "Walked all day . . . / Scrambling through dust down Tamalpais . . . / Two of us, carrying packs." He adds, "From Siwash strawberry-pickers in the Skagit / Down to . . . / . . . this whole spinning show . . ." ("Burning, 15"). The poet as hero has gained a kind of existential knowledge: all will be "transformed." And he offers this "boon," his vision, to the reader. Thus, the poem itself becomes an offering. In this poem, as Campbell's study suggests, there is a sense of resolution which makes the continuing quest possible. Each separation is a rehealing. One journey only marks the spot for additional exploration.[13]

II *"the mythical method"*

After viewing primitive cave paintings, it is said, T. S. Eliot returned home and composed "Tradition and the Individual Talent." Whether apocryphal or not, such an action seems more in character for Gary Snyder than for T. S. Eliot. Nonetheless, upon closer scrutiny, striking resemblances exist between the work of the younger and older poet. Possibly, Eliot's response, his feelings of awe, reverence, and admiration for the art treasures of the Paleolithic past indicate the point at which these seemingly disparate poets touch. The similarity, as a colleague has indicated, lies in their essential archaism, primitivism, and mysticism.[14] To this list, may be added their conservatism.

In "Tradition and the Individual Talent," Eliot writes: "Tradition is a matter of much wider significance. . . . It involves, in the first place, the historical sense, which we may call nearly indispensable to anyone who would continue to be a poet beyond his twenty-fifth year; and the historical sense involves a perception, not only of the pastness of the past, but of its presence. . . . This historical sense, which is a sense of the timeless as well as of the temporal, is what makes a writer traditional. And it is at the same time what makes a writer most acutely conscious of this place in time, of his own contemporaneity."[15] In the terms outlined by Eliot, Snyder's perception is "historical." In *Myths & Texts* and in *Mountains and Rivers Without End* (to be discussed), the richness of archaic culture underlies the images of the destruction and decadence of the present era. Quite "traditional" in this respect, Snyder's work manifests his awareness of his place in the stream of events called "time."

Eliot and James Joyce were among the first to explore and to exploit artistically the new consciousness discovered by psychology and anthropology. "The Waste Land" in particular, contains much specialized and esoteric information of this sort. In his notes on "The Waste Land," Eliot admits his indebtedness to those who have gone before him.[16] In the same way, and with similar modesty, Snyder acknowledges his own debt to Eliot. In a recent letter he writes: "of course studied Eliot, much too — very carefully."[17] But, as might be expected, Snyder saw in Eliot's work not only a similar fascination with anthropology and psychology but also the model of a new style and technique for the exploration and exploitation of these psycho-authropological materials. This method Elizabeth Drew has called Eliot's "mystical vision" and "mythical method."[18]

In reviewing James Joyce's *Ulysses*, Eliot writes, and Snyder quotes in his Reed College thesis: "In using the myth, in manipulating a continuous parallel between contemporaneity and antiquity, Mr. Joyce is pursuing a method which others must pursue after him. They will not be imitators. . . . It is simply a way of controlling, of ordering, of giving a shape and a significance to the immense panorama of futility and anarchy which is contemporary history. . . . Instead of narrative method, we may now use the mythical method."[19] This myth consciousness and the desire to form a new social mythology through the use of literature was Snyder's intention while writing *Myths & Texts*. His thesis, written just prior to the creation of *Myths & Texts*, indicates his profound interest in cultural regeneration in the sections where he digresses from his analysis of the Haida swan-maiden myth and theorizes about the nature of poetry and the role the poet should play in society. His respect for the views of Jung, Campbell, Wheelwright, Eliot, and others in regard to the implications of the function of myth is obvious.

In this respect, there are also striking similarities between "The Waste Land" and *Myths & Texts*. The general purposes of each work are similar, and both works were written during a time of excessive materialism and expansion brought about by the unrestrained application of technology. Both assess the psychic health of an era after a period of war and social upheaval. Many sections, even particular lines, are alike. As Ernest Hemingway once said, and Robert O. Stephens paraphrases in a recent article on the influence of Stendhal on Hemingway, ". . . indebtedness is a challenge. One borrows materials or models to surpass, not to equal or to imitate."[20] Possibly, this explains why *Myths & Texts* seems at times to parody the earlier work. In *Myths & Texts*, Snyder employs and adapts to his own needs the themes, technique, and general purpose of "The Waste Land"; and, as a result, he produces a work similar in content and in style, if radically different in spirit. Certainly, if not the màtrix, in Stevens' terminology, "The Waste Land" might be seen as the paradigm of *Myths & Texts*.

In *Myths & Texts*, Eliot's presence is found most obviously when comparing his sections III and V in "The Waste Land" to Snyder's "Burning." Eliot's sections I, II, IV, with their sense of illicit love, sterility, guilt, and shame contrast to the generally lusty and psychically uncomplicated drift of *Myths & Texts*. In section III, "The Fire Sermon," Eliot alludes to Buddah's so-called "fire sermon"; one of the more neurotic "sermons" attributed to the Buddah, it is almost prudish in its admonitions. Snyder, seemingly aware of this irony, responds in "Burning" to Eliot's reference in lines 196–98 of "The Waste Land" to Greek mythology — to Diana caught naked by Actaeon. Snyder, in "Burning" takes a humorous turn on the reference: "Actaeon saw Dhyana in the Spring. / it was nothing special, / misty rain on Mt. Baker, / Neah Bay at low tide" ("Burning, 13"). One can see that Snyder studied Eliot closely, so much so that he employed not only Eliot's "mythic vision" and "method" but also specific materials — and in this instance, turned what displeased him to his own ends. Or, in other terms, Snyder accepted Eliot's challenge. The matter-of-factness of Snyder's reply to "The Waste Land" in his use of the reference to Diana is refreshing. Also interesting in this respect is Snyder's use in "Cartagena" (*Riprap*) of the statement by St. Augustine, quoted by Eliot on line 307 of "The Waste Land." Snyder's poem is about a visit to a Columbian brothel. The poet cries, as did St. Augustine, "Cartagena! swamp of unholy loves!" Nonetheless, Snyder accepts the truth of the Buddah's sermon. That is, the senses satisfy, but are not to be trusted.

As "Burning" 2 and 3 indicate, both poets are aware of the existence of the void and the transience of sentient life, but other specific points of similarity are also evident. The final lines of Eliot's "The Fire Sermon" may be a source for the last section of *Myths & Texts*, "Burning." In these lines by Eliot, there is a similar sense of purgation and abandonment: "Burning burning burning burning / O Lord Thou pluckest me out / O Lord Thou pluckest / burning.[21]" Also, Snyder's use of the place name Thunder Creek in "the text" and "the myth" of "Burning" may be a coincidence of geography. Yet, there are other numerous points of comparison between "Burning" and another section from "The Waste Land," "What the Thunder Said." Eliot writes "Of thunder of spring over distant mountains" (1. 327). "Here is no water but only rock / . . . dry sterile thunder without rain" (11. 331–42). Although Eliot concludes this section and the poem with the words, "Datta. Dayadhvam. Damyata. / Shantih shantih shantih," suggesting acceptance and consequent peace, it is not convincing, so full of remorse and cynicism is this poem, so unlike the later peace and acceptance of "Ash Wednesday." One may compare the macabre quality of "The Waste Land" with its lamentations and hallucinations to the satisfying ending of *Myths & Texts*. Although the Fisher King remains sterile and cannot set his lands in order, the "creative hero" in *Myths & Texts* offers hope. Snyder writes in "Burning, 17, the text":

> Toward morning it rained
> We slept in mud and ashes,
> Woke at dawn, the fire was out,
> The sky was clear. . . . (*Myths & Texts*, 47)

And in "the myth":

> Rain falls for centuries
> Soaking the loose rocks in space
> Sweet rain, the fire's out
> The black snag glistens in the rain. . . . (48)

In contrast, "The Waste Land" seems dated, exhibiting the cynicism of the decade after World War I. In Snyder's terminology, Eliot's response to "the text" is reticent; his "myths" guilt-ridden. Snyder seems to suggest that Eliot has become introverted, having lost his faith in mankind. Such is Snyder's non-Christian response to Eliot's "challenge."

Yet, although the tone of the two poems and the sensibilities of each poet differ, and although "The Waste Land" is essentially an urban poem that is concerned more with the fate of "civilization" than with the future of *homo sapiens* as a species, the influence of Eliot's poem on *Myths & Texts* cannot be denied. Both works are apocalyptical, for they deal with the destruction of the world as man once knew it. In Eliot's case, the world is that of "civilized man" before World War I; in Snyder's, the world of primitive man before the coming of "civilization." Both poems are concerned with the change in values, the loss of faith, and the lack of reverence for life. And, finally, both poets draw on many cultures, archaic and contemporary, in an effort to create a mythology through which culture may redirect its energies in more spiritually productive ways. In other words, Eliot and Snyder are moralists. They attempt to reorient and save modern man from himself. Both poets are, in the highest sense, religious poets.

III   *"and cut down their groves."*

When reading *Myths & Texts*, it is important to understand the central metaphors which unify the work: logging, hunting, burning; for, since Snyder's associations for these terms are unconventional, these words may create misconceptions unless they are discussed. Although a neutral term for the average reader, "logging" has come to represent for Snyder the mindless rapaciousness of society and the destruction which has occurred due to man's egoistical manipulation and exploitation of his environment. This theme Snyder explores in later poems, in his essays, and in the broadsides

"Smokey the Bear Sutra" and "Four Changes." "Hunting," in contrast to its practice by weekend tourists in the mountains for a shot at a deer, is an act of worship for Snyder. If undertaken with knowledge, full awareness, and reverence, the hunt, in contrast to logging, represents the communion of all life forms and the participation of man in his eco-system. Hunting makes clear man's place in the food web. To hunt and then to eat the flesh of the slain animal is in Snyder's words, "making love with animals" (*Earth House Hold*, 119).

As for "burning," Smokey the Bear, boldly painted on government posters, has come to represent to most Americans the prevention of forest fires ("Only *you* can prevent forest fires!"); and although the near-sacredness of this practice is strongly maintained by lumbering interests, many ecologists have realized the necessity of naturally caused forest fires. In contrast to the position of Smokey the Bear and his human allies, who continue to stamp out fires indiscriminately, burning in Snyder's work is a cleansing force. Through "a hot clean / burn" (*Manzanita*, 22), trash is eliminated and energy released.

In "Smokey the Bear Sutra," Snyder changes Smokey's image by radicalizing him. Militantly, Smokey indicates the task to his followers — later called "Fellow Dharma Revolutionaries" by Snyder — to "fearlessly chop down the rotten trees and prune out the / sick limbs of this country America and then burn the leftover / trash." Unlike the response of T. S. Eliot in "The Waste Land," burning to Snyder does not represent punishment for sin. Snyder interprets the physical data of life differently, for he does so without guilt or remorse. Thus, burning does not represent destruction in the conventional sense; it is more correctly seen as reconstruction or as restructuring in the mind of Gary Snyder. In short, the central metaphors in *Myths & Texts* structure the work and artistically display the evolution of an alternate mythology, as the following discussion of the individual sections should indicate.

As Lynn White, Jr., has written in "The Historical Roots of the Ecologic Crisis," man has acted under the false impression that nature was his to exploit in any way he wished.[22] *Myths & Texts*, written in the early 1950's, was one of the first poetic works to respond to such thinking. According to Snyder, *Myths & Texts* is his "most ordered and complete" work,[23] while to Thomas Parkinson the book is a "sacred text."[24] Having been a logger himself, Snyder is intimately aware of the mentality to which White refers. In one sense, so Snyder relates, *Myths & Texts* was written to deal with his own complicity in the destruction of America. Snyder, like the cartoon character, Pogo, learned that the "enemy" is not someone else; it is himself. In writing *Myths & Texts*, Snyder states that he was "looking for that thing in the American character which would, like Ahab in *Moby Dick*, search the globe for something in order to destroy it.[25]

"Logging" is concerned with the causes of this destruction on the deepest human level, the unconscious mind. In "Revolution in the Revolution in the Revolution," Snyder states:

We must pass through the stage of the
"Dictatorship of the Unconscious" before we can
Hope for the withering-away of the states
And finally arrive at true Communionism. (*Regarding Wave*, 39)

And in his essay, "Buddhism and the Coming Revolution," Snyder speaks of ignorance "which projects into fear and needless craving" (*Earth House Hold*, 90). He continues: "The soil, the forest and all animal life are consumed by these cancerous collectivities; the air and water of the planet is being fouled by them" (91). What Snyder is referring to in these lines is developed poetically in "Logging"; for, as he relates in Poem 5, "Again the ancient, meaningless / Abstractions of the educated mind" (*Myths & Texts*, 7) are the cause of the destruction of the forests. Thus, Snyder asks in Poem 10, "What bothers me is all those stumps: / What did they do with the wood?" (11). In Poem 4, the destruction is described:

A thousand board-feet
Bucked, skidded, loaded —
(Takasago, Ise) float in a mill pond:
A thousand years dancing
Flies in the saw kerf. (6)

Poems 2 and 14 answer the question, "What did they do with the wood?". Poem 2 begins with a prefacing quotation from the Bible which Snyder has called in a public reading, "instructions to our ancestors": "But ye shall destroy their altars, / break their images, and cut down their groves. / *Exodus* 34:13."[26] This poem relates that

> San Francisco 2 × 4s
>   were the woods around Seattle:
> Someone killed and someone built, a house,
>   a forest, wrecked or raised
> All America hung on a hook
>   & burned by men, in their own praise. (4)

And Poem 14 forcefully informs the reader that

> The groves are down
>   cut down
> Groves of Ahab, of Cybele
> Pine trees, knobbed twigs
>   thick cone and seed
>   Cybele's tree this, sacred in groves
> Pine of Seami, cedar of Haida
> Cut down by the prophets of Israel
>   the fairies of Athens
>   the thugs of Rome
>   both ancient and modern;
> Cut down to make room for the suburbs. . . . (14)

In Poem 8, Snyder describes logging and vividly displays its hidden consequences to other life forms:

> Thick frost on the pine bough
> Leaps from the tree
>   snapped by the diesel
>
> . . .
> The D8 tears through piss-fir
> Scrapes the seed-pine
>   chipmunks flee,
>
> A black ant carries an egg
> Aimlessly from the battered ground.
> Yellow jackets swarm and circle
> Above the crushed dead log, their home.
> Pitch oozes from barked
>   trees still standing,
> Mashed bushes make strange smells. (9–10)

This poem depicts a landscape of ruin; the unseen effects on other levels of existence are made clear. Through the language of the

poem, especially the verbs, the poignancy of this senseless destruction is emphasized. The poem makes the reader feel that logging is
more than a matter of economics, by imaginatively recreating this
act of desecration. Ten years later in *Earth House Hold*, Snyder
states: "(Rape of the world: destructiveness of Western civilization.
Those insane Spaniards in Central America — answering to abstractions of gold and religion. The nature, wildlife, Indian life, Missis-
sippi, Grand Canyon, didn't move them. The whole Western
hemisphere a gift to Spain from the Pope)" (54–55).

On the other side of this seemingly "hard-nosed" response to
ecological conditions is Snyder's mythologizing of nature in an effort
to create an alternate state of consciousness. Poem 1 of "Logging"
begins with a description of the lustiness of the archaic May Day:
"Young girls run mad with the pine bough . . ." (4). In this poem,
Snyder plays with a theory of psychoanalytical anthropologist Geza
Roheim. When Snyder writes that "The May Queen / Is survival of /
A pre-human / Rutting season'," he is suggesting the existence of
Stone Age, human sexual periodicy. In *Myths & Texts*, Snyder
searches the roots of human behavior; and in Poem 12 the reader
sees Snyder's respect for the American Indian is for his mythic
consciousness and close contact with his environment:

> I ought to have eaten
> Whale tongue with them.
>   they keep saying I used to be a human being
> "He-at-whose-voice-the-Ravens-sit-on-the-sea."
> Sea-foam washing the limpets and barnacles
> Rattling the gravel beach
> Salmon up creek, bear on the bank,
> Wild ducks over the mountains weaving
> In a long south flight, the land of
> Sea and fir tree with the pine-dry
> Sage-flat country to the east. (13)

These lines present the primitive's mythological apprehension of
reality,[27] and this state of consciousness is what the poet seeks to
assume in his role of mythmaker and, subsequently, to develop in
the reader. In this poem, Snyder recreates the Indian's awareness of
the sacredness of all life forms; and the reader is made to feel this
pre-logical, pre-scientific mode of consciousness.

This more intimate relationship to nature is also evident in Poems

3 and 15 of "Logging." In these poems there is a sense of connection that is mystical in essence, but is also pragmatic and concrete. Here is Snyder's reverence for the lodgepole pine and its "wonderful reproductive / power . . ." (5). Symbolizing the cyclic aspect of nature in its ability, like the mythic phoenix, to resurrect itself from the ashes, the lodgepole pine points the way to a new view of nature. Quoting Pa-ta Shan-jen, the Chinese painter who "lived in a tree" and watched a great dynasty crumble, Snyder concludes the "logging" section. Suggesting this wider view of man's activities in the face of endlessly evolving nature, Snyder quotes, " ' The brush / May paint the mountains and streams / Though the territory is lost' " (15).

IV "— *I think I'll go hunt bears.*"

It is interesting to note that the term "hunting" is derived from the Persian word for paradise and signifies a hunting ground or park which includes animals, for such is the feeling created in section II of *Myths & Texts.* The contrast between sections one and two is striking since the intimate relationship only pointed to in "Logging" is participated in in "Hunting." The sense of communion with nature which is lost when the groves are cut down is regained artistically in "Hunting." In particular, "Hunting" reintroduces the reader to "the magic of animals," affecting intimate connection with them. To hunt is to participate directly in the lives of animals and to realize dependency upon them. "There is a great truth in the relationship established by hunting," Snyder writes, "like in love and art, you must become one with the other" (*Earth House Hold,* 139).

A psychoanalytical anthropological theory even states that the roots of religion are found embedded in hunting magic. Snyder writes in "Poetry and the Primitive": "To hunt means to use your body and senses to the fullest: to strain your consciousness to feel what the deer are thinking today, this moment; to sit still and let yourself go into the birds and wind while waiting by the game trail. Hunting magic is designed to bring the game to you — the creature who has heard your song, witnessed your sincerity, and out of compassion comes within your range" (*Earth House Hold,* 120). Hunting, then, as human activity, is juxtaposed against logging, which symbolizes the irreverent, the ignorant, and the wasteful. In contrast, hunting represents the knowledgable, mindful, and economical. When properly undertaken — that is, with reverence, love, and full awareness — hunting to Snyder is holy and sacred.

In this second section of *Myths & Texts*, Snyder hatches his new myth (Poem 1, "first shaman song") and poses his cultural alternative that is reconstructed from the archaic past. He does so by presenting the lives of animals and their significance to man. In "Hunting," the reader learns to know, love, and respect these "people" for what they are. His consciousness is changed; he can never respond again to animals as stereotypes since they become more than recreational "resources." As Snyder has said, all animals have the "Buddha-nature" or, in Western terms, are alive and have souls. Thus, in "Hunting, 2," Snyder begins to develop a new cosmology by linking man and animal, hunter and hunted. In this poem hunters prepare for the kill which will enable them to live:

> Atok: creeping
> Maupok: waiting
>   to hunt seals.
>
> The sea hunter
>   watching the whirling seabirds on the rocks
>
> The mountain hunter
>   horn-tipped shaft on a snowslope
>   edging across cliffs for a shot at goat. . . .
>
>   (*Myths & Texts*, 18)

Men and animals, of course, have much in common. Not only do they share the same biosphere, they are also, as the poem above suggests, mutually interdependent — they are sources of energy for each other. In addition, animals, in certain ways, are extensions of mankind; or, more specifically, they manifest certain human-archetypal experiences in their behavior. Birds, for example, can fly. With ease, they enact an age-old dream of man, possibly taking its roots in some dim remembrance of floating in the ambionic fluid of the womb. In "this poem is for birds," man's unconscious life is evoked:

> Birds in a whirl, drift to the rooftops
> Kite dip, swing to the seabank fogroll
> Form: dots in air changing line from line,
>   the future defined. (19)

The flight of birds is an image which pulls and tugs, moving something deep inside man. This image is similar to the image of "the Mandala of Birds" in Snyder's poem "The Hudsonian Curlew," now collected in *Turtle Island*. A sense of augury emanates from the last two lines. This strikes an archaic note, which is fulfilled at the end of the poem in the lines: " — the swifts cry / As they shoot by, See or go blind!" Man's connection with birds as seers and teachers is completed with the multiple meaning of "See." The poem suggests that all nature is a source of knowledge.

In Poem 4, which further develops the poet's interest in "the flying people," Snyder pulls together many of the myths of the Indians of the Pacific Northwest concerning birds. Citing mythical birds believed to possess magical powers, Snyder writes:

> Phoenix, hawk, and crane
> owl and gander, wren,
> Bright eyes aglow: Polishing clawfoot
> with talons spread, subtle birds
> Wheel and go, leaving air in shreds
> black beaks shine in gray haze.
> Brushed by the hawk's wing
> of vision. (20–21)

In this poem, the poet mythologizes these creatures, exhibiting man's awe of birds. In "Migration of Birds" in *Riprap*, Snyder had already suggested how inner-directed birds are; in addition, they are peaceful and give joy with their color, songs, and antics; and, as if by magic, they can fly. In this poem, he expands the significance of birds by painting them bigger than life and by replacing man's old values and modes of perception. As a result the reader learns to "see" differently.

Clearly, Snyder's poetic treatment of animals illustrates the sense of the significance that man has seen and has artistically invested in them. In Snyder's work, as in the archaic past, animals have become manifestations of man's psychic life — projections of its drives and fears. Man's close observation of animals has always shown him much of interest about himself; and, in this respect animals such as the bear and the deer assume great significance for Snyder. In Poem 6, "this poem is for bear," Snyder introduces the reader to a mixture of archaic bear mythology from the forests of Siberia:

> A tall man stood in the shadow, took her arm,
> Led her to his home. He was a bear.
> In a house under the mountain
> She gave birth to slick dark children
> With sharp teeth, and lived in the hollow
> Mountain many years.
>   snare a bear: call him out:
>
> honey-eater
> forest apple
> light-foot
> Old man in the fur coat, Bear! come out!
> Die of your own choice!
> Grandfather black-food!
>   this girl married a bear
> Who rules in the mountains, Bear! (22)

The bear is powerful and kingly, and was often depicted in Indian tales as a father-figure. Jaime de Angulo's *Indian Tales,* which Snyder reviewed, offers a good example in this respect.[28] In *Indian Tales,* "Bear" and "Antelope" are the father and mother, respectively. To the Indian, the bear was also a minor deity; it looked like a man. Farther back into the dim shadows of the Paleolithic, the Bear cult conducted the oldest known ritual observances. And in the nineteenth century a tremendous amount of bear lore developed. The frontiersman tested his strength and courage against that of the bear. The bear is still associated with manhood.[29]

In *Myths & Texts,* Snyder also uses the ancient mythological figure of the trickster. Functioning as the all-wise creator-sufferer who has seen and knows it all, the trickster, in this case in the form of "Coyote," is the supreme practitioner of one-upsmanship. Acting in the fashion which his name implies, the trickster always gets the last word. Coyote is beyond birth and death, and is at the same time commentator, participant, and creator. As Snyder writes in "Hunting, 16," ". . . beasts / Got the buddha-nature / All but / Coyote" (31). Since in myth the trickster may take the form of raven, hare, spider, or other animals, the trickster is a paradoxical figure. In fact, the character of Han-shan in Snyder's "Cold Mountain Poems," and, at times, the public figure, or "mask" of Snyder himself are evocations of the trickster. Snyder even extends the trickster's characteristics to hobos and other subculture types. Actually, the trickster possesses no well-defined form, and thus Snyder may give it the widest application in his life and works.

In short, the trickster, Coyote, is a god-like but somewhat shabby creature, who, nonetheless, is responded to readily and is respected. In Snyder's review of *Indian Tales*, he states, while discussing at length the figure of Coyote, that it is "the most important, and surely the most enigmatic character in the book . . ." (*Earth House Hold*, 30). In this poetic employment of this ancient psychic structure, one sees the workings of Snyder's mythopoeic imagination. Possibly depicting man's struggle with himself and his world, Coyote is a projection of him and of his search for self-knowledge. In *Myths & Texts*, Snyder uses this mythologized creature to embody and dramatize the extreme states of human consciousness.[30]

In *Myths & Texts*, the deer also becomes the subject of art; he dramatizes psychic experience and gives shape to dream. In "this poem is for deer" ("Hunting, 8"), this function is made clear:

> Deer on the autumn mountain
> Howling like a wise man
> Stiff springy jumps down the snowfields
> Head held back, forefeet out,
> Balls tight in a tough hair sack
> Keeping the human soul from care. . . . (25)

In this poem the poet tells how he "Missed a last shot / At the Buck" (24), but on another occasion, how someone, possibly the poet, while driving under the influence of alcohol, saw and shot it:

> Pull out the hot guts
> with hard bare hands
> While night-frost chills the tongue
> and eye
> The cold horn-bones.
> The hunter's belt
> just below the sky
> Warm blood in the car trunk.
> Deer-smell,
> the limp tongue. (25)

In terms of the previous discussion, the killing of the deer in this poem seems needless and stupid; for, an act of ego, it was not initiated by love or necessity, as the poet knows. His psychic state is evident in his response, "shot / That wild silly blinded creature down" (25); for the poet seemingly blames the deer for man's temerity. Certainly, the poem in general and the third stanza in particular do not depict the deer as a silly creature. To the contrary, the poet sees it as a beautiful, magical animal. It is man, when hunting without full self-knowledge and reverence, who is "silly." Thus, as if to assuage the guilt and remove the stain of man's act, the poem ends with a bit of Indian hunting magic. This kill is an act of sacrilege; and thus, in terms of the mythic dance of the hunt, the deer will not wish to die for the poet-hunter: "Deer don't want to die for me" (26). The poet must purify himself, as the Indians did before him, by drinking seawater as an emetic. The poet will mortify himself: "Sleep on beach pebbles in the rain / Until the deer come down to die / in pity for my pain" (26).

Hunting itself is a kind of dance in which on many levels our destiny, biological and psychic, is worked out and expressed in symbolic movements. Dance is, in a sense, the enactment of process, the acting out of destiny. The dancer dances, locked as if in trance into the sequence of steps which lead to the inevitable conclusion. On another level, deer are often associated with dance and with creation mythology. In the poem discussed above, Snyder allows the deer to speak. Effectively mythologized, the deer states:

> "I dance on all the mountains
> On five mountains, I have a dancing place
> When they shoot at me I run
> To my five mountains" (24)

This poem suggests the "dance" of the hunter and hunted, the movement which leads to the death, to consumption, and to rebirth as energy in new form.

In Hindu mythology, one finds the notion of the world-creating dance as expressed by expanding form; for the Hindus believe that the world was created through dance. When American Indians dance, miming the movement of animals, they believe that the animal's spirit speaks through them. To Susanne Langer, who discusses in "Virtual Powers" the illusion of the powers projected in dance,[31] dance is more than rhythmic movement, ballet, sculpture, or drama; it is symbolic form. More specifically, the dance is a vivid representation of a world seen, imagined, and given shape in dance. In this respect, the themes of hunting, dancing, and eating are closely related in Snyder's work; for, as the ancient Chinese proverb relates, "Nothing belongs to you until you have eaten it." The theme of food and eating — first stated in "Hunting," developed in *Mountains and Rivers Without End* ("The Market") and *The Back Country* (notably in "How to Make Stew . . .," "A Berry Feast," "Oysters"), and referred to in *Earth House Hold* — is completed in *Regarding Wave*. Through these works, the theme moves toward its completion and fulfillment in "Song of the Taste" in which the objective fact of existence, that men and animals are mutually creating each other, is made manifest (*Earth House Hold*, 129). Searching for man's place in the food web, which Snyder calls ". . . the vast 'jewelled net' which moves from without to within" (*Earth House Hold*, 129), he asks, "just where am I in this food-chain?" (*Earth House Hold*, 32). In "Song of the Taste," the poet adores and mythologizes food, making the reader feel and know deep inside the connection between man and meat, love, life, and death. The poet writes,

> Eating each other's seed
> > eating
> ah, each other.

> Kissing the lover in the mouth of bread:
> > lip to lip. (*Regarding Wave*, 17)

Hunting, therefore, is to Snyder "The re-enactment of a timeless dance: [here and now, co-creating forever] . . ." (*Earth House Hold*, 134). It is an act, related to eating and dancing, of participation and communion for the continuation of the species. The steps of the hunt — stalking, killing, eating, growing, procreating, and dying — recapitulate the cycle of life. Clearly, as indicated in Poems 14 and 16, where hunting is regarded as an act of compassion, hunting operates on another level other than energy transferral. To Snyder, hunting is sacramental.

V *"The sun is but a morning star"*

Section three of *Myths & Texts* provides the resolution or consummation that has been worked toward in "Logging" and "Hunting." As the "first shaman song" in "Hunting" announces the coming of spring — the beginning of the cycle of life appropriate to the hunting section — the "second shaman song" in "Burning" foretells summer, the end of the life cycle, and thus its continuation. In the spring song, the high-country snow melts; the river rises; and a sense of hope, promise, and fertility prevails. In the summer song, the river recedes: "Limp fish sleep in the weeds / The sun dries [the shaman] as I dance" (34). This sense of heat and drought is intensified by the imagery of solidification:

> Still hand moves out alone
> Flowering and leafing
> > turning to quartz
> Streaked rock   congestion of karma
> The long body of the swamp.
> A mud-streaked thigh. (34)

The shaman's summer song is appropriate to the "Hunting" section it follows, for it deftly introduces and establishes the tone of the final section of *Myths & Texts*, "Burning," which it precedes. As in primitive ritual, the shaman's song gives form to psychic knowledge. In his trance, the shaman envisions the changes which will occur: the hand will turn to rock (quartz), and the swamp recede. Soon the pond will be like a mud streak on the earth's thigh, an almost unnoticed stain on the earth's surface. This is the working out of natural processes, the transformation of energy. Stated in Buddhist terms, it is the "congestion of karma." In this poem, existence is described in terms of process; that is, in terms of states of energy — temporarily solidified, or in obvious transformation. The poet's awareness of the constancy and immutability of change in everything is presented by relating natural substances to parts of the human anatomy, seeing both as "waves," or moments of frozen energy. As science has made clear, strictly speaking, there are no objects; there is no substance. Everything is dynamic. Because of limited human perception, men see substance where there is actually slow but gradual change. Thus, as stated in "second shaman song," there is a very significant analogy, an important connection between "the long body of the swamp" and "A mud-streaked thigh." In this poem, man is inexorably and completely a part of the process of energy transformation. The last section of *Myths & Texts*, "Burning," suggests that this is a physical reality we cannot avoid.

The search for wisdom is a significant theme in "Burning," and it is related to the acceptance of the fact discussed above. In *Myths & Texts*, different methods of achieving such enlightenment are explored: Poems 3 and 5 relate the search for wisdom through the use of drugs; in Poem 5, the smoking of jimson weed is described: " 'Don't kill it man, / The roach is the best part' " (37). The experience is unsuccessful, however; for the poet still experiences "an incessant chatter." The drug offers only a brief diversion, similar to drunkenness:

> great limp mouth
> hanging loose in air
> quivers, turns in upon itself,
> gone
> with a diabolical laugh (37)

In Poem 3, however, the "dark drug-death dreams" lead to a temporary opening of the "doors of perception": "inturned dreaming / Blooming human mind / Dropping it all, and opening the eyes." Next, Poem 8 offers the model of the famous enlightenment experience that the naturalist John Muir had while climbing Mt. Ritter. Snyder puts Muir's prose into poetic form. Caught on a cliff, Muir relates,

> My mind seemed to fill with a
> Stifling smoke. This terrible eclipse
> Lasted only a moment, when life blazed
> Forth again with preternatural clearness.
> I seemed suddenly to become possessed
> Of a new sense. My trembling muscles
> Became firm again, every rift and flaw in
> The rock was seen as through a microscope,
> My limbs moved with a positiveness and precision
> With which I seemed to have
> Nothing at all to do. (39)

Affected, as he relates earlier in the poem, by a "doom" which "Appeared fixed," it is obvious that Muir experienced what in Zen is called *kensho*, or brief enlightenment. He became for a moment one-minded, and his senses became preternaturally acute. He could act spontaneously, without thought: for a time, he was beyond culture, beyond the entanglements of language. Consequently, Muir lived more fully than ever before while faced with death on Mt. Ritter.

The search for enlightenment and the relationship of the steps taken in its achievement continue in other poems. In Poem 10, after the statement in Poem 9 of the social games he has played, the poet, descending a mountain with pack animals, offers the vow of the Bodhisattva (a kind of Buddhist saint) that he will not accept complete enlightenment, and thus the end of suffering, until all other living beings are saved. Like Maitreya, the mystical future Buddha of Poem 4 who, it is believed, will be born in a grove of flowers and preach for sixty-thousand years until all reach enlightenment, the poet identifies his search with that of others: "He will not go, / But wait . . . / Til flung on a new net of atoms: / Snagged in flight / Leave you hang and quiver like a gong / Your empty happy body / Swarming in the light" (36).

Poem 11 describes *zazen* (sitting meditation), another means for gaining enlightenment. After relating the Zen *koan* (philosophical question) and its answer, Snyder sits, meditates: "Ingather limbs, tighten the fingers / Press tongue to roof / Roll the eyes" (41). He awaits enlightenment, which is described in terms of metamorphosis: "In the dry, hard chrysalis, a pure bug waits hatching" (41). Following this poem, Poem 12 relates the sequence of three terrible meditations which the poet experiences. And then, in Poem 13, the poet turns with Zen-like humor the serious quest for enlightenment upon itself with the finality of a smack on the back given by the *jikijitsu* (meditation hall monitor). He states, "(What's this talk about not understanding! / you're just a person who refuses to see)" (43).

In this final section "Burning," the poet-hero achieves enlightenment and returns with his boon. The vision of ceaseless change, or energy transformation, is the knowledge he offers. In *Myths & Texts* Snyder confronts this new knowledge of time, space, and constant change; and he accepts their profound implications. Of his awareness, he writes in "Burning, 2":

> One moves continually with the consciousness
> Of that other, totally alien, non-human:
> Humming inside like a taut drum,
> Carefully avoiding any direct thought of it
> Attentive to the real-world flesh and stone. (34)

As Snyder relates, men live in the void: "Forms within forms falling / clinging. . . ." But, accepting this fact, he concludes in this poem, originally titled "Changes: 3":

> "have no regret —
> chip chip
>   (sparrows)
> & not a word about the void
> To which one hand diddling
> Cling (35)

Or, as Snyder states in Poem 6,

> Granite rots and crumbles
> Warm seas & simple life slops on the ranges
> Mayflies glitter for a day
> Like Popes!
>
>   where the sword is kept sharp
>   the VOID
>   gnashes its teeth (38)

In Poem 13, he relates, "It's all Vagina dentata / (Jump!) / 'Leap through an Eagle's snapping beak' " (44). Here the poet suggests the metaphorical leap into the void that is beyond nihilism and that transcends the ego. As stated in Poem 9, this "leap" is "surrender into freedom . . ." (40). In terms which strike closer to home, the poet writes:

> "Earthly Mothers and those who suck
> the breast of earthly mothers are mortal —
> but deathless are those who have fed
> at the breast of the Mother of the Universe." (39)

As this poem indicates, Snyder's conception of life is nonhumanistic; for man is not seen as the center of the universe. When men read Snyder, they must rethink their accepted conventions; for, to Snyder, man is simply

> A skin-bound bundle of clutchings
>   unborn and with no place to go
> Balanced on the boundless compassion
> Of diatoms, lava, and chipmunks. (44)

Clearly, man is becoming, a changing process. What form "human" energy will take a million years from now no one can say. As Snyder states,

> "What is imperfect is best"
>   silver scum on the trout's belly
>   rubs off on your hand.
> It's all falling or burning —
>   rattle of boulders
>   steady dribbling of rocks down cliffs
>   bark chips in creeks. . . . (46)

As the trickster-creator figure Coyote relates, ending Poem 16, "Earth! those beings living on your surface / none of them disappearing, will all be transformed (47)." As the noted anthropologist Loren Eiseley has written, men are eyewitnesses to evolution as much at this moment as if they had lived three hundred million years ago. We need only to open our senses.[32]

In this regard, the burning metaphor which unifies this final section functions effectively. Actually, all change is combustion in its widest sense; it simply occurs at different rates, and it is often imperceptible to the human eye. Moreover, fire is not only a destroyer but, in essence, a preserver (similar to the Hindu god Shiva, whom Snyder refers to). Many species of plants can germinate only after a fire. In the case of the lodgepole pines mentioned in the discussion of "logging," their cones require not only heat to open but fire-cleared soil, high in minerals, to germinate. Thus, capturing this cyclic nature of life, Snyder writes in "Burning, 15":

>   lightning strikes, flares
> Blossoms a fire on the hill.
> Smoke like clouds. Blotting the sun
> Stinging the eyes.
> The hot seeds steam underground
>   still alive. (46)

And he concludes *Myths & Texts* by quoting Thoreau, "The sun is but a morning star" (48).

Myths & Texts has no sense of an ending, for it projects Snyder's belief in the vastness and in the enormous potentiality of the future. There is a constant setting forth in *Myths & Texts* in the sense of Whitehead's intellectual "adventures."[33] There is insistence on the possibility of hope since life is a mutually interrelated becoming. In *Myths & Texts* Snyder makes no judgments because no ultimate standards are set. The only absolute is change. Like Whitehead,

Snyder's concern is the perpetual examination of the fundamental notions concerning the nature of reality. As Charles Altieri has noted, Snyder has developed "a lyric style which itself embodies a mode of consciousness leading to a state of balance and symbiotic interrelation between man and his environment."[34] Thus, for Snyder, the ". . . reconciliation of opposites is possible for all because the reconciliation need not be imposed; it exists in fact."[35] In "Burning" in particular, Snyder is objective and calm; but he is affirming the processes of nature in the face of man's destructive tendencies. His concern is healing and recuperation, and his voice is raised in benediction.

CHAPTER 5

The Nature of History and the Quest for Wisdom

A N old Chinese saying relates that, even though the nation is defeated, the mountains and rivers remain the same. This strong "sense of place" and connection with nature rather than with the polity is captured in the Chinese word for landscape which consists of two characters meaning "mountains" and "waters." Begun in 1956, *Mountains and Rivers Without End*, like the mountains and rivers it describes, is a continuing work. It is Snyder's *magnum opus*. Originally, Snyder believed that this long poem would unroll forever and be like the Chinese sideways scroll paintings after which it is modeled. "It threatens to be like its title," he stated in 1959.[1] In *The Dharma Bums* (1958), novelist Jack Kerouac quotes an excited Japhy Ryder, a thinly veiled version of Snyder, who is relating his plans for what at that time was called "Rivers and Mountains Without End":

I'll . . . just write it on and on on a scroll and unfold on and on with new surprises and always what went before forgotten, see, like a river, or like one of them real long Chinese silk paintings that show two little men hiking in an endless landscape of gnarled old trees and mountains so high they merge with the fog in the upper silk void. I'll spend three thousand years writing it, it'll be packed full of information on soil conservation, the Tennessee Valley Authority, astronomy, geology, Hsuan Tsung's travels, Chinese painting theory, reforestation, Oceanic ecology and food chains.[2]

Although this quotation is exaggerated and somewhat over-enthusiastic in the manner typical of Kerouac's transcriptions of conversations with his friends, it does capture both the monumental scope of the work and Snyder's conception of it. As early as the late 1950's, Snyder's plan was quite specific: the structure and major concerns of this work — the search for wisdom and the exploration of the nature of history — in addition to particular subjects and individuals to be included, such as the Chinese Buddhist wanderer Hsuan Tsung [Hiuan Tsang], were determined. This optimistic project, of course, will not continue forever. Only as a completed work of art will *Mountains and Rivers Without End* gain a kind of immortality. Within the next two or three years, Snyder hopes to complete the work which will contain approximately forty sections.[3] Then, he relates, he will turn to "a series of Hymns to Logic and Ecstasy in their play with the inter-relatedness of myriad phenomena."[4]

So far, Snyder has completed thirteen sections of *Mountains and Rivers Without End;* for he has published approximately one section a year since 1961. Two phases can be seen in the development of this work: the first, which runs from 1956 to about 1966, includes seven sections; the second, from 1968 to mid-1976, covers so far six sections. The work as a whole grew out of Snyder's own quest for wisdom; and as a result, the sections, display for the most part his state of mind and his spiritual achievement at the time of composition. With a few exceptions, notably "Bubbs Creek Haircut" and "The Market," the sections composed since 1966 are generally more controlled, sustained, and conceptually forceful; for the years between 1966 to 1969 were of great consequence to Snyder.

Much occurred during these years, and he made important decisions which altered the course of his life. For example, 1966 is the date of the publication of Snyder's collected poems, *A Range of Poems.* Also in that year he completed his formal Zen studies upon the death of his teacher, Oda Sesso. In 1967, while experimenting with communal living at the Banyan Ashram on Suwa-No-Se Island off the coast of Japan, he married his wife Masa. And late the following year, after the birth of his first son and the publication of *The Back Country,* Snyder returned to this country. His collected prose, *Earth House Hold,* was at that time at the publishers, and it appeared in the spring of the next year. Since this time, Snyder has re-rooted himself in the American West. The early, more youthfully intense stages of his quest have ended; and Snyder, in his maturity, now considers himself in the role of poet-shaman; he is dealing with the American's debt to the Indian and is applying Buddhist thought and practice to this problem in particular and to life in the West in general.

The first edition of *Mountains and Rivers Without End,* containing six sections, was published in 1965 by Four Seasons Foundation.

It included "Bubbs Creek Haircut," first published in 1961; "The Elwha River" (1961); "Night Highway Ninety-Nine" (1962); "Hymn to the Goddess San Francisco in Paradise" (1963); "The Market" (1964); and "Journeys" (1965). Not included in the original edition, but published in *Poetry* (December, 1966) was "Three Worlds / Three Realms / Six Roads," another section from *Mountains and Rivers Without End* which will be included in the final edition. This section is similar to the work of the early 1960's and should be placed in that period. In *Poetry* (March, 1968), Snyder published "Eight Songs of Clouds and Water" and included in it is a poem entitled "The Rabbit."

When these "Songs" were published in 1969 and again in 1970 in *Regarding Wave*, "The Rabbit" was not included. It is intended for a place in the final version of *Mountains and Rivers Without End*. This poem marks the beginning of the second phase (1968–mid-1976) in the development of *Mountains and Rivers Without End*. Since "The Rabbit," Snyder has published five more sections. In 1970 *Six Sections from Mountains and Rivers Without End Plus One* was published by Four Seasons Foundation in conjunction with the Phoenix Bookshop. This limited edition included, in addition to the earlier sections, "The Blue Sky" (1969). Subsequently, Snyder has published "The Hump-Backed Flute Player" (*Coyote's Journal* #9); "Ma" (*Coyote's Journal* #10); "Down" (*Iowa Review*, I [1970]); and "The California Water Plan" (*Clear Creek* #8, November, 1971; republished in *The Fudo Trilogy*, 1973).

I   *"a superb framework"*

As Snyder has indicated, the dramatic structure of *Mountains and Rivers Without End* "follows a certain type of *Nō* play."[5] Snyder has admirably adapted this Japanese form and its conventions to the American Western experience and to his own artistic and psychic needs, particularly in regard to Snyder's quest for wisdom and in his desire to deal with the plight of the American Indian. As Orientalist Donald Keene states, "The Nō provides a superb framework for a dramatic poet. It is in some ways an enlarged equivalent of the tiny *haiku*, portraying only the moment of greatest intensity. . . ."[6] Like *haiku*, *Nō*, bare, simple, and impressionistic, relates the momentary and the timeless, the personal and the historic. In the fourteenth century, Seami (1363–1444) and his father Kwonami developed *Sarugaku no No* into its present form, for they established the standards of the structure, the content, and the sentiment of *Nō*. According to Seami, *Nō* must relate a simple story which is easy and dignified; it should include chanting and dancing, accompanied by flute music; it should be direct in style; and it should offer "words of good wish."[7] By contemporary dramatic standards a *Nō* production is sparse; it has few characters, conventionalized properties, and an unchanging landscape. *Nō* was integrated into Buddhist ritual, and up to six different types of plays were produced at festivals. One type, the warrior play, is relevant to this discussion and will be treated presently. Basically constructed around the journey motif, each series of plays began with the actor naming himself, relating his origin and destination, and singing a "song of travel."[8]

While in Japan in 1956, Snyder referred to his intended adaptation of *Nō* and to speculations concerning the possibility of an "American Nō stage," which might have "background painting a desert and distant mountains? chorus on a long low bench. Maybe one large real boulder" (*Earth House Hold*, 37). More than five hundred years before, Seami had written, "If a writer wishes to make a new play — one that does not use an existing story — he should bring in some famous place or ancient monument. . . ."[9] Undoubtedly, the locale for Snyder's "new play" became the American West.

Mentioning the *Nō* and its traditional concerns, Snyder, in *The New American Poetry*, delineates the two major themes, quite similar to those of *Nō*, of *Mountains and Rivers Without End:* "Travel, the sense of journey in space that modern people have lost . . . and the rise and fall of rock and water. . . . [and] History and its vengeful ghosts."[10] Earlier in this statement, Snyder had written, "I tried to make my life as a hobo and worker, the questions of history and philosophy in my head, and the glimpses of the roots of religion I'd seen through meditation, peyote, and 'secret frantic rituals' into one whole thing. As far as I'm concerned, I succeeded."[11]

Throughout *Mountains and Rivers Without End* the journey motif ("song of travel" of *Nō*) is evident. However, it is most apparent in the first six sections and in "Three Worlds." The specific source in this regard is the *Nō* play *Yamauba* by Seami. In this work, where the title "Mountains and Rivers Without End" finds its inception, "hills," meaning mountains, represent life; and one's travels in these hills, in terms of the Buddhist "Wheel of Life," are the endless round of reincarnations. In Snyder's journal notation for September 1, 1965, composed while backpacking in the Cascade Mountains, he states. "Nō play *Yamauba* — forever walking over mountains; over mountains — red leaves falling — striking through winter snowstorms — spring sticky alder buds — summer bees. J. sees me wandering way off ahead. And when she catches up says, 'You're already spoken for. . . . you belong to the mountains' . . ." (*Earth House Hold*, 94–95).

In this quotation, one sees Snyder's attempt to mythologize his own life; but, more importantly, one notices the grasp which the *Nō* travel motif had in 1965 on his consciousness. This archetype of physical and psychic journey provides both subject matter and structure for the early sections of *Mountains and Rivers Without End*. The picaresque quality of *Mountains and Rivers Without End*, with its Oriental overlay, appears quite obviously in "Night Highway Ninety-Nine." In this poem, Snyder identifies with hobos and all fellow spiritual travelers, as he says elsewhere, who are in search of the Dharma. Describing a hitchhiking trip from northern Washington to San Francisco, the "holy city" of the "Beats" glorified in "Hymn to the Goddess San Francisco in Paradise" (possibly a caricature of Christian's "Celestial City" in Bunyan's allegory *Pilgrim's Progress*), the poet states,

> — Chinese scene of winter hills & trees
> us "little travellers" in the bitter cold
> (*Mountains and Rivers Without End*, 25)

Three stanzas later, one reads:

> The road that's followed goes forever;
> In half a minute crossed and left behind. (25)

II   "'Passage to more than India!'"

Although the poet generally describes his journeys in terms of physical trips, there can be no doubt that they are essentially psychic. As in "Journeys," the wilderness topography of the American West and that of the unconscious mind are synonymous. In this poem, in which the description of visions and physical journeys alternate, the poet "kept a chart of our route in / mind" (*Mountains and Rivers Without End*, 38). In "Bubbs Creek Haircut," "The Elwha River," and "The Market," Snyder plays with time and place in his psychic journey; for he is fooling with remembrance and recall and with moving freely and without comment between the past, present, and future. Whether sitting in the barber's chair or cutting a trail in the high Sierra, as he relates in "Bubbs Creek Haircut," all actions are the same, all one in mind. It is, "out of the memory of smoking pine" (*Mountains and Rivers Without End*, 11). Thus, Snyder, hauntingly evoking Ernest Hemingway's "Big Two-Hearted River," can refer to the Elwha as a "dream / river" (*Mountains and Rivers Without End*, 12), and write of "Lost things" as if they are somehow not lost forever.

In "Three Worlds / Three Realms / Six Roads," Snyder offers autobiographical images that display the stops along the route of his journey from civilization to wilderness, from Occident to Orient, and from childhood to maturity. Taking six roads, or paths, he has seen different worlds and experienced various realms of existence. The stages in the poet's change of consciousness are clear, and Snyder's approach to psychic exploration is typically practical. More important than time or place, however, is method. In "Three Worlds," he indicates "Things to Do" to provide the methodology for consciousness-expansion and psychic development. He states, "Keep moving — move out to the Sunset — / Get lost / Get found."[12]

In its individualism, lusty sensuality, and optimism, "Three Worlds" reminds the reader of the poetry of Walt Whitman. As critics such as Robert Bly and Thomas Lyon have noted, there is much in common between the works of Whitman and Snyder;[13] and some similarities between these two men in character and sensibility also exist. Snyder, who acknowledges this stylistic and spiritual affinity, refers to Whitman as one of his "poetic mentors."[14] Similar to the Whitman of *Leaves of Grass*, one sees in "Three Worlds" and in *Mountains and Rivers Without End* Snyder's identification with all things. Like Whitman, Snyder makes no value judgments; he sees the unity behind all seemingly separate life forms and affirms them. *Mountains and Rivers Without End*, too, is like *Leaves of Grass*, Snyder's *magnum opus*; for this work is the "one whole thing" to which Snyder refers, as noted earlier in this discussion.

The mysticism of Whitman and Snyder, their "cosmic consciousness," and the spiritual drift of their writing are the main points of
comparison. However, another equally significant connection is
evident, for Snyder is obviously one of the "new breed of poets
. . . interpreters of men and women and of all events and things"
predicted by Whitman in his Preface to the 1855 edition of *Leaves of
Grass*. [15] In addition, heeding Whitman's call to native genius, first
made in the Preface, Snyder looks away from Europe when he is
searching for his own roots. In "Journeys II," he writes:

> Through deep forests to the coast,
> and stood on a white sandspit looking in:
> over lowland swamps and prairies
> where no man had ever been
> to a chill view of the Olympics, in a chill clear wind.
>   (*Mountains and Rivers Without End*, 38)

Also like Whitman, Snyder hopes for a more perfect America. His
awareness of America's mission and his deep concern for its spiritual
progress are clearly evident in *Mountains and Rivers Without End*.
Similar to the Whitman of *Democratic Vistas*, Snyder accepts the
"lessons of variety and freedom." [16] He affirms Whitman's belief in
democracy, and he regards Whitman's "varied personalism," the
"full play for human nature to expand itself in numberless and even
conflicting directions," [17] as the only hope for the real progress of
Americans. "The Market," in which Snyder relates that all life forms
and processes are equal ("= fresh-eyed bonito, live clams" — 35),
explores this belief extensively. Snyder also describes this concern
in his essay "Passage to More than India." The title is taken from
Whitman's poem, "Passage to India," which praises voyages of discovery which join mankind in brotherhood. In his essay, Snyder
discusses the continuous existence of what he calls the "Great Subculture," which is, roughly speaking, a manifestation of Whitman's
"varied personalism." Snyder states that, without diversity and
freedom, a culture atrophies and becomes violent. Like Whitman
before him, Snyder calls for an end to debilitating materialism, for
more open relationships between people, and for a sacramental
relation to life in general.

In "The California Water Plan," a recent section of *Mountains
and Rivers Without End*, Snyder condemns what he considers the

needless and desecrating damming of rivers. Expressing these feelings, he quotes Buddhist scripture: "'Up the sandy trail in a sacred way we come'" (*The Fudo Trilogy*). Snyder and Whitman argue, as Snyder puts it, "that man's life and destiny is growth and enlightenment in self-disciplined freedom . . ." (*Earth House Hold*, 105). Only when men are free and "have the full right to live to their limits," as Snyder states in "Smokey the Bear Sutra" (now included in *The Fudo Trilogy*) will men "enter the age of harmony of man and nature. . . ." Concluding the essay by quoting Whitman, Snyder presents spiritual progress in terms of the journey of the soul:

> "Passage to more than India!
> Are thy wings plumed indeed for such far flights?
> O soul, voyagest thou indeed on voyages like those?"
>
> (*Earth House Hold*, 112)

Both as poets and mystics, Whitman and Snyder record their personal voyages of spiritual discovery; but their concerns go beyond themselves. As cataloguers of the adventurous quest for spiritual knowledge and as singers of the health and "inner" progress of their nation, they more properly assume the role of psychic historians and shamans.

III *"our Karma as Americans"*

Since 1968, Snyder has been increasingly more concerned with the questions of history and the plight of the American Indian. *Mountains and Rivers Without End* and the intent and course of its development are evidence of this deepening of interest. As implied in the previous discussion of Whitman, the quest for wisdom and wholeness becomes in Snyder's later work the search for roots, and thus the exploration of American history. An early example of this type of spiritual archeology, known to Snyder, is the *Kojiki*, a most ancient Japanese work, completed in 712 A.D., that traces the origins of modern Japan. Its title means "Record of Ancient Things," and it is very possible that Snyder has had this work in mind during the writing of the more recent sections of *Mountains and Rivers Without End*.

Written under the auspices of the imperial court, the *Kojiki* is an

impressive historical as well as literary document. Attempting to
establish authoritative genealogies, the *Kojiki* compiled myths,
legends, historical narratives, songs, and folk etymologies; de-
lineated the heavenly and earthly deities; related the reigns of em-
perors and the journeys spreading culture; and documented quite
interestingly the pacification of the earlier peoples and their surrender of the land. In regard to Snyder's purpose in writing *Mountains
and Rivers Without End*, the *Kojiki* seemingly offered him the
example of a work which, attempting to obtain a definitive text,
displayed unintentionally yet graphically the less than laudatory
history and directions of a nation.

To the historian Henry Adams, writing at the turn of the century,
history could be explained in terms of sequence. In "The Dynamo
and the Virgin," a chapter from his famous autobiography, *The Education of Henry Adams* (1906), Adams stated his "dynamic theory of
history" — the idea that the essential law of history is the sequence
of force. He identified this energy with sexuality and fertility. Fifty
years before, Whitman had poetically made the same statement in
Leaves of Grass. In "A Backward Glance O'er Travel'd Roads" written at the end of his career, Whitman "reaffirmed the sexual bias of
his book"; and, in the words of his editor, James E. Miller, Jr.,
Whitman ". . . surely knew, as Henry Adams recognized, that in
his sexual vision he had focused on a neglected historical force that
was central to the human experience."[18] In short, for Whitman, the
"law" of history was procreation. In certain ways, Snyder's view of
history as process is similar to the dynamism of Adams and Whitman.

To the Mahayana Buddhist (Madhyamika School) such as Snyder,
the phenomenal world is insubstantial: nothing itself has substance.
As the center of an onion reveals, there is only relationship. This
concept is Nagarjuna's doctrine of "emptiness" which Hsuan Tsang
carried from India to China in the seventh century A.D. (and which
is discussed in Section IV of this chapter). Through the eyes of a
Buddhist such as Gary Snyder, the sequence of human endeavor,
what is called "history," becomes simply the working out of conditions or relationships. In this respect, another Buddhist doctrine,
that of "karma," is relevant; for, as defined by Zen Buddhist and
teacher Philip Kapleau, "karma" is "action and reaction, the continuing process of cause and effect." To Kapleau, "Thus our present
life circumstances are the product of our past thoughts and actions,

and in the same way our deeds in this life will fashion our ... mode of existence."[19]

By loosely applying this doctrine to the contemporary situation in America, and particularly to suppressed minorities like the Indians, Snyder makes his concern with history specific. In an interview conducted by Bruce Cook and printed in *The Beat Generation*, Snyder relates that the Indian first led him to the Orient;[20] and the Indian has seemingly led him back. In an earlier "conversation" with Dom Aelred Graham in Kyoto in 1967, Snyder indicated that his "original teacher" had been the American Indian;[21] and, in his response to Cook some three years later, he stated:

I think the Indians are going to show us the next stage of this other culture. But of course if we had only looked before, they could have shown us earlier. We really had such an opportunity to learn from them . . . .

No, the Indians certainly didn't see the best of the white race. And all this — the Indians and what we did to them — it's coming back to us, you see. It's our Karma as Americans.

Well, in simpleminded terms it means that when you've done something wrong to someone or something you have to pay them back. And it has to do with the idea that one of the ways an obligation of this sort is discharged is by becoming like that which has been wronged.[22]

In view of this statement, one can understand not only Snyder's regard for the historical but also his present focus on the condition of the American Indian. In a section entitled "The Redskins," in his essay "Passage to More Than India," Snyder refers to the "invisible presence of the Indian," to their "human history" and "Older powers" which he feels are becoming evident (*Earth House Hold*, 108). For Snyder, the Indian plays the difficult dual role in American history of teacher and of victim. As the model of primitive ecology and religious responsibility, as living embodiment of mythic consciousness and preserver of a tradition which values psychic life, and yet as scapegoat and victim of the American drive for "manifest destiny" and "progress," the paradoxical situation of the Indian in American history is both perplexing and tragic.

Again, drawing on his knowledge of the *Nō* in an effort to deal with the white man's complicity in genocide and the destruction of Amerindian culture, Snyder adapts the convention of the warrior-play in which the ghost of the dead warrior speaks so that it may rest. In a typical Japanese warrior-play, *Ikuta*, by Zembo Motoyasu

(1453–1532), a man-child, whose origins are obscure, yearns in adolescence to meet his father, Atsumori, who was slain in battle. Instructed in a dream to go to the woods of Ikuta, the boy makes this journey; and he meets in the forest the ghost of his father who, according to the conventions of the warrior-play, relates the tale of his people's flight and ultimate annihilation in the woods of Ikuta.[23]

The similarity between the condition of Atsumori and his people and the American Indian is obvious. Both Atsumori and the Indians were driven from their lands, and both groups were finally destroyed and scattered by their enemies. And, as in *Ikuta*, which Snyder has read, the poet allows the ghost of the defeated to speak in *Mountains and Rivers Without End*, in order artistically and ritualistically to release the spirit of the Indian and thus allow the "new" Indian to be reborn. In "The Hump-Backed Flute Player" in particular, the poet refers to his sense of "obligation" in regard to the Indian: "Ah, what am I carrying? What's this load?"[24] Then he conjures up the pathetic ghost of the Indian Jack Wilson, called "Wovoka," who in the late nineteenth century had a vision at Walker Lake, Nevada. Wovoka prophesied that, if the Indians danced the "Ghost Dance," they would become invulnerable to bullets and that the dead buffalo would rise up and crush the white oppressor. However, as Snyder makes evident, Jack Wilson and the Indians, like the warrior Atsumori and his people, were overcome by an enemy more warlike and powerful than they. Through Snyder's cross-cultural adaptation of this dramatic form, he deals with the white man's guilt and opens the way for the next stage of the development of Indian culture.

Understanding of and commitment to the Indian and his way of life, as indicated above, is certainly a central aspect of Snyder's work. In this respect. Snyder has stated: "We won't be white men a thousand years from now. We won't be white men *fifty* years from now. Our whole culture is going someplace else. The work of poetry is to capture those areas of the consciousness which belong to the American continent, the non-white world. . . ."[25] This "world of mythology and intuitive insight that belongs with primitive culture . . . ," of which Snyder speaks later in this statement, is what he suggests that Americans get "back in touch" with. Obviously, Snyder has learned much from the Indian which has significantly shaped his life-style and his imagination. The misty figure of the Indian and his archaic past stands behind many of Snyder's poems.

"Through the Smoke Hole" in *The Back Country* offers a good example of this use of the Indian, because Hopi Indian cosmology and symbology provide the basis for the poem. Interestingly, Hopi mythology projects a definite evolutionary sense, even offering a glimpse of their migration as a people from the Asian land mass thousands of years ago. The Hopi have a strong sense of place, both cultural and ecological. In "Through the Smoke Hole," one finds the sense that the Indian has of the continuity of life — the ceaseless growth and development, the spiraling outward toward new forms. In this poem, Snyder uses as a focus the Hopi architectural structure of the *kiva*, the round underground ceremonial room in the pueblo in which rituals are held to insure the enduring continuity of the community, and to bridge the gap between life and death. The *kiva*, meaning the world below, symbolized for the Hopi the womb of Mother Earth. As Frank Waters states in *Book of the Hopi*, "a small hole in the floor symbolically led down to the previous underworld, and the ladder-opening through the roof symbolically led out to the world above."[26] Since this ladder symbolized the reed up which man climbed during his emergence from the lower forms of life, the concept of the multi-level, or multi-world universe is preserved in the symbolism of the *kiva*. The Hopi believed that there were four successive worlds and, significantly, that movement between them was possible.

The symbolism of the *kiva* and the cosmology of the Hopi has obviously caught Snyder's poetic imagination. The value the Indian places on psychic life and his belief in the existence of many worlds support Snyder's Buddhist conception of multi-leveled "reality" and of the necessity of visiting other mental realms. The *kiva* with its smoke hole becomes a convenient metaphor for focusing the psychic quest; for, as Snyder indicates, "There is another world above this one; or outside of this one; the way to it is thru the smoke of this one, & the hole that smoke goes through. The ladder is the way through the smoke hole; the ladder holds up, some say, the world above; it might have been a tree or pole; I think it is merely a way" (*The Back Country*, 110). The different "worlds" of the Hopi and the many levels of the universe, represent for Snyder, in popular psychological terminology, the "doors" of perception or, more specifically, the levels of consciousness. In "Through the Smoke Hole," the transience and arbitrariness of modern life and its attention to material rather than to spiritual goals become obvious. As the poem states, "It is possible to cultivate the fields of our own world without much / thought for the others" (110). The Hopi and the American Indian in general, with their supporting culture, have a sense of place and knowledge of psychic life, and they manifest, therefore, a civilization from which the white man could have learned a great deal. Instead, Snyder suggests, he chose to destroy it.

Recent sections of *Mountains and Rivers Without End* mark Snyder's shift in emphasis back to the topography of the American West and indicate his deepening concern for the mutual plight of white man and Indian. In "Down," Snyder, as if announcing a return to his roots, returns "Back to where it started." "Down" links with and extends the earlier sections of "Three Worlds" and "Journeys." Looking over that cliff once again, Snyder relates "I swallow, lean forward, look down: / My balls and belly turn over." Asking, "can I make it?," Snyder jumps unaided — "Ah, gone off" — and reaches "stars!"[27] Prior to the publication of "Down," "The Rabbit," like Ko-san in "Journeys," led the poet back to the mountains and rivers of the American West. This "grizzled black-eyed," trickster-like figure, drawn from Amerindian mythology, tells the poet the source of the water which nourishes those roots: "the / mountains and juniper / Do it for men. . . ."[28]

It is in "Ma," one most fully hears the Indian speak.[29] Through the use of the convention of the epistle, specifically a letter reputedly found by Snyder in an abandoned shack in the mountains near his home, the reader learns much about the Indians' strength of character and their ability to survive under difficult conditions. Written by the mother of an Indian boy who has taken a job far away from home, this poetic letter reports everyday events and bits of gossip to her son. She writes about wages, the cost of clothing, the domestic animals, the garden, and the activities of friends and relatives. She also offers advice about saving money, being careful, and not drinking too much. Beneath this seeming trivia is the existence of abject poverty, cultural isolation, ignorance, and degradation. There is no money, no gun; people are dying; a relative is killed in Vietnam; the cattle are falling off; and friends are moving away. Ma is resourceful and courageous, but she is resigned. Lacking the cultural tradition which sustained her people for thousands of years and finding herself caught in a capitalistic democracy, the Indian can only attempt to endure. As Ma writes, "Indians are always drinking then dieing. / Don't seem to mind tho."

IV   *"the poet-shaman"*

The poet Robert Bly has written that Snyder "is a poet who might be called devout, or religious in the most elementary sense."[30] And this observation goes to the heart of *Mountains and Rivers Without End*, for Snyder's central purpose is certainly religious. As he writes in "Without," recently included in *Turtle Island* (1974), his concern is "healing / not saving." Unlike the clerics of the past, Snyder waves no hymn books, offers no dogma, and does not attempt to convert the Indians. His concern is cathartic and therapeutic. Like Whitman and Robert Duncan, another contemporary poet whom Snyder respects, Snyder has assumed in *Mountains and Rivers Without End* the role of shaman, the psychic healer; and in "The Hump-Backed Flute Player" and in "The Blue Sky" (1969) one watches his swirling dance.[31]

Something should be said here about Shamanism. First, it is one of the oldest and most widespread forms of religion; it is still practiced by certain primitive peoples. Second, and more important, Shamanism is concerned with behavior rather than with belief. Essentially, it is directed toward healing and maintaining the conditions which will insure the health and continuation of the group. The central figure of shamanistic ritual, the shaman, is usually born with psychic difficulties; but, through curing himself or being cured by another, he develops a profound folk knowledge of the unconscious mind. In a very real sense, the shaman is the first poet; he expresses, through the incantations he sings and the visions of his trance which he reports, the anxieties of the group. Giving shape or form to the unconscious life of his people, giving it imagery — essentially through the act of naming — the shaman exorcises mental disorder and heals psychic wounds. In the light of these powers, the reader can understand Snyder's concern for developing this primitive function of the poet.

In "Poetry and the Primitive," Snyder states that "The Shaman-poet is simply the man whose mind reaches easily out into all manners of shapes and other lives, and gives song to dreams" (*Earth House Hold*, 122). Snyder, who has seen the natural and universal connection between singing and healing, has "set himself to train it. . . ." To Snyder, therefore, "Poetry *is* Shamanism."[32] In short, the poet and shaman are men of knowledge and thus of power. They see what others do not; but more importantly, because they articulate this knowledge, they empower or energize others and restore them to psychic life. As a result, the poet's roles of "creative hero," psychic historian, and poet-shaman blend. At this point, the historical and religious levels of *Mountains and Rivers Without End* interrelate.

In this respect, a distinct connection can be made between the shaman "OLD MAN MEDICINE BUDDHA" referred to in "The Blue Sky" and Hsuan Tsang and Kokopilau in "The Hump-Backed Flute Player." All are religious figures, mental physicians, and psychic practitioners; or, according to Snyder's definition, they are poet-shamans. The figure of "OLD MAN MEDICINE BUDDHA" is a syncretism, for Snyder fuses the archetypical elements from Buddhism and Amerindian culture. A bit of explanation seems necessary, since the "Buddha" is the enligthened one — the "TATHAGATA," or "suchness" mentioned in the poem, and since the element of "medicine" refers to "white" or to psychological magic. To the Indian, "medicine" was not something to be ingested; rather it was anything which brought psychological power, anything which made one whole. The term "medicine man" is often misused today, for it meant in Amerindian culture the man of knowledge, the healer, or the shaman.

The character Hsuan Tsang in Snyder's "The Hump-Backed Flute Player," is such a medical practitioner, in the sense of the word as used above. Hsuan Tsang was a Chinese who in 629 A.D. traveled from China to Nalanda University, the great center of Buddhist culture in India. As Snyder's poem relates, Hsuan Tsang's journeys were long and perilous; but he returned to China with religious texts, icons, and relics. Carrying "sutras" (religious texts) in his pack with a parasol on top, Hsuan Tsang spread the Buddhist doctrines of Nalanda throughout China. Especially significant is the fact that Hsuan Tsang had been taught Nagarjuna's "Doctrine of the Void," the concept already discussed above that nothing exists of itself; there is only relationship. Thus, Snyder writes, "he carried / 'emptiness' / he carried / 'mind only'." To Snyder, Hsuan Tsang was a liberator and healer because the doctrine he spread gave intellectual form to unconscious knowledge, and thus had the power to free men's minds from useless suffering.[33]

Hsuan Tsang and Kokopilau are alike in Snyder's mind. Kokopilau, the Amerindian petroglyph of a hump-backed flute player which appears chiseled on rock walls throughout the South-western United States and into Mexico, is associated with the end of the Pleistocene era and is generally thought to symbolize fertility and the coming of spring. It is believed that the hump on his back is a pack full of seeds which he sows as he travels and that the flute music creates warmth. In a sense, both Hsuan Tsang, the historical figure, and Kokopilau, the image of a minor Amerindian deity, spread seed. Kokopilau brings rebirth; Hsuan Tsang, enlightenment.[34]

The major concern of Shamanism was healing. As Snyder relates, "The purpose of California Shamanism was 'to heal disease and resist death, with a power acquired from dreams' " (*Earth House Hold*, 123). Through their visionary experiences that enable them to transcend ego and society, Hsuan Tsang, "OLD MAN MEDICINE BUDDHA," and the poet himself gain the power to heal. In "The Hump-Backed Flute Player," Snyder's vision brings all levels of creation and consciousness to synthesis. He ascends through the spiraling forms of Amerindian culture, Buddhism, Kundalini yoga, and the flora, fauna, and topography of the American West to the stars and then back. Traveling through and beyond several cultural exteriors,[35] the poet-shaman returns with his vision and states that "up in the mountains that edge the Great Basin / it was whispered to me / by the oldest of trees." Like Hsuan Tsang, the poet learns and passes on to the reader that

> spiral, wheel
> or breath of mind
>
> *desert sheep with curly horns.*
> *the ringing in your ears*
> *is the cricket in the stars.*

In "The Blue Sky," vision is gained through the ingestion of psychotropic herbs, such as morning glory and cannabis, and through incantation. The ritualistic nature of the poem, proper in the circumstances it describes, is evident. In the first stanza, the motif of psychic journey and quest is established: " 'Eastward from here, / . . . there is a world called / PURE AS LAPIS LAZULI' / . . . it would take you twelve thousand summer vacations / driving a car due east all day every day / to reach the edge of the Lapis Lazuli realm. . . . "[36] As in taking a "trip," in the contemporary usage of the term, the poet chooses a color and fixes his mind on it.

In the second stanza, he explores the meaning of "Blue"; and the poem becomes a kind of etymological chant. This magical use of language, similar to the shaman's song, releases the secrets of matter and mind locked in the roots of words. As in the recent "Magpie's Song" from *Turtle Island*, where the shamanistic bird states, "Here is the mind, brother / Turquoise blue. / I wouldn't fool you." "No need to fear / What's up ahead / . . . be at rest" (69), its singing makes one whole: "*Heal*. hail whole . . . ."[37] Reading much like a transcription of a primitive religious observance, "The Blue Sky" shows that Snyder has gone back to the root of language and poetry. Exploring the visionary realm of the shaman-poet, he has created a kind of contemporary *mantra* (simple, repetitive chant). As he states in 1966, "If the poem becomes too elliptical it ceases to be a poem in any usual sense. Then it may be a *mantra*, a *koan*, or a *dharani*. To be used as part of a larger walking, singing, dancing, or meditating practice."[38] Thus language, or song, becomes "medicine."

Exploring all the possibilities of blue, similar to following a vein through rock, the poet weaves through cultural boundaries in the six sections which follow. Like the figure of the hump-backed flute player, Kokopilau, which adorns the pages of "The Blue Sky" and separates its sections, the shaman-poet follows the thread of his mind and pursues his vision, exploring the nature of healing and referring to hallucinogenic herbs which, now banned by law, were once considered "medicine," or bringers of vision:

> Glory of morning
>   pearly gates, the
>   heavenly [blue].[39]

In the final section of the poem, the shaman-poet achieves ecstasy. The poet becomes huge; his perspective, boundless. In this state of non-ordinary consciousness — one similar to Carlos Castaneda's "Separate Reality," — "Impurities flow out away to west, / behind us, *rolling*."[40] The experience is timeless, and the poet exists without a body. Ending his chant and moving beyond the confines of language, the shaman-poet can only repeat "The Blue Sky / The Blue Sky / The Blue Sky" before he soars, like the eagle, out of sight.

One cannot say what new directions, if any, *Mountains and Rivers Without End* will take. Although thirteen sections have been written at this date, many more are planned. However, Snyder has said that the "kick-off" for the final section will be mountain-man Jim Bridger's famous comment, "Where there ain't no Indians that's where you find them thickest."[41] And Snyder has referred to the narrative of the sixteenth-century Spanish explorer Cabeza de Vaca, who in his *Adventures in the Unknown Interior of America* (1542), wrote about the hospitality of the Indians of the Southwest and the magnificence of their culture. From all indications, therefore, additional explorations into the obliteration of a race and the destruction of their culture should be forthcoming. Nonetheless, enough sections have been completed so far to outline the thematic structure and the basic stages of development of the work as a whole. Certainly, Snyder's purpose seems set and his sources and analogues determined. From the early preparations of "Bubbs Creek Haircut" to the epiphany of "The Blue Sky," Snyder acts out his psychic quest for wisdom, explores the nature of history, and expresses his karmic concern for the Indian. It will be interesting to see where this long work takes Snyder.

CHAPTER 6

Into the Back Country

I *"Our world of snow and flowers"*

EMERGING from a tradition rooted in westward expansion and in the frontier experience of the nineteenth century — the West of Jed Smith and Jim Bridger, and of writers such as Joaquin Miller, Mark Twain, John Muir, and Jack London — Snyder's work offers a vivid example of what might be considered as Western literary imagination.[1] Such a perception of the world is direct, nonintellectualized, mythic, and often mystical. In essence, it is naturalistic; for, atagonistic to civilization and "progress," this view stresses a profound reverence for the wilderness and for its personal and social value.

Although familiar with the works of many of the already-mentioned writers, Snyder's most direct connection with the Western literary imagination comes through the poetry of Robinson Jeffers (discussed in Chaper 8) and, more importantly the poetry of Kenneth Rexroth. An adopted Westerner who in 1921 at age sixteen had traveled in boxcars from the Midwest to San Francisco, Rexroth quickly recognized the inherent power and beauty of the Western landscape. In the 1920's he began to write poems about his backpacking trips into the pristine wilderness. In "A Living Pearl," a poem written thirty years later about work in the mountains, he writes that "Half my life has / Been passed in the West, much of it / On the ground beside lonely fires / Under the summer stars, and in / Cabins where the snow drifted through / The pines and over the roof."[2]

Rexroth's motif of life in the mountains, logging, rounding up wild horses, cutting trail, or simply rambling alone for days was adeptly nurtured and developed by him. He was one of the first poets to concern himself with the psychological reality of man in the wilderness; he made the preliminary connections between wilderness and mind. His example illustrates the truism that it is often the outsider who shows the natives what there is to see.

In certain respects, Rexroth's wilderness poetry seems to have served as a guide for Gary Snyder. It offered a realizable paradigm of life-style, one with which Snyder was somewhat familiar; but, more importantly, it offered the example of an older poet who had focused these wilderness experiences in the interest of art. Rexroth's work vividly illustrated that the poet must write about what is closest; and, in the West, this subject is wilderness. Snyder's "Bubbs Creek Haircut" and possibly the first six sections of *Mountains and Rivers Without End* in which this poem is collected seem influenced by Rexroth. As in Rexroth's "A Living Pearl," Snyder's subjects are the joyous preparations for summer working on a trail crew in the Sierra Mountains, the worker stories and lingo, the remembrances of past jobs, the evocations of lusty life in the wilderness.

In addition to Rexroth's cognizance of the artistic value of the wilderness experience, he was also aware of the difference between the earlier Northeastern perception which dominated American nature writing for two centuries and that of the West. Although conversant with various Romance languages and deeply knowledgable about European culture, Rexroth turned away from the model of traditional Romantic nature poetry and looked west to China. The form of Chinese nature poetry, essentially Buddhist, rejected abstraction and dichotomy; and it seemed, therefore, a more fitting frame for capturing the wilderness experience. Rexroth's translations from the Japanese and Chinese were to influence other West Coast poets as well as Snyder. who fondly remembers the regular Friday evenings in the early 1950's when he and other poets spent evenings reading and discussing poetry in Rexroth's apartment. Snyder has mentioned recently that Rexroth was "ornery at times" and difficult for many to get along with, but that he liked and respected Rexroth, especially his "sense of civilization" and his awareness of the significance of the Indian in the American consciousness.[3]

In a recent interview, Snyder made explicit this respect for Rexroth's pioneering work. Rexroth is "A great reclaimer,"[4] stated Snyder. Such admiration, however, was also felt by Rexroth for the younger poet. Early in Snyder's career, Rexroth was to speak highly

of Snyder and his work. Most recently, in his discursive, but insightful *American Poetry in the Twentieth Century*, Rexroth was to write
that "Snyder is the best informed, most thoughtful, and most articulate of his colleagues." He is "an accomplished technician . . . who
has developed a sure and flexible style capable of handling any
material he wishes."[5] Ultimately, Snyder dedicated *The Back Country* to Rexroth, as if affectionately paying his debt — a professional
and intellectual one.

Undoubtedly, Rexroth would consider many of Snyder's poems in
Riprap and *The Back Country* as prime examples of what he has
called "bear-shit-on-the-trail" poetry. For Rexroth, in effect, is the
creator of this subgenre of nature poetry that is Chinese in esthetic
quality but also indigenous to the American West. Although Rexroth considers Snyder the foremost practitioner of this type of writing, Rexroth was one of the first poets in the twentieth century to
develop the guidelines of what might also be called "mountain
poetry." Its characteristics are not complex; the poem, of course,
has a wilderness setting; the poet is the actor and speaker in the
poem and is usually alone, or at least solitary in observation and
thought.

In this type of poem, there is usually a reference to a star in order
to orient both poet and reader. Flora and fauna are recorded, usually pines and wild flowers, deer, bear, trout, and the birds which
fly or hop past the poet. The specific locale is often picturesque —
near a cold, clear lake or creek, or at the foot of a snowy peak. And
the reader is given a sense of the beauty, relative permanence, and
superiority of the wilderness in contrast to the machinations of men,
which, as the poet states with relief, are far, far away. In "Mid-
August At Sourdough Mountain Lookout," Snyder describes the
heat, the pitch glowing on the fir-cones, the flies swarming across
the rocks and meadows, and then writes:

> I cannot remember things I once read
> A few friends, but they are in cities.
> Drinking cold snow-water from a tin cup
> Looking down for miles
> Through high still air. (*Riprap*, 1)

In this "mountain poem," Snyder offers the reader a picture of
solitariness and serenity. Living simply and close to nature, the poet
is at peace. In "August on Sourdough, A Visit From Dick Brewer,"

Snyder was to develop again this same theme. After the short visit, Brewer leaves wearing the poet's rain gear, "flapping in the wind / Waving a last goodbye half hidden in the clouds / To go on hitching / clear to New York . . ." (*The Back Country*, 25). Although Snyder is happy to see an occasional visitor, he mentions "Me back to my mountain and far, far west," with obvious relief, satisfaction, and the pride of possessiveness.

In another poem, Snyder describes his work cutting brush in "Trail Crew Camp At Bear Valley":

> trail a thin line through willow
> up buckbrush meadows,
> creekbed for twenty yards
> winding in boulders
> zigzags the hill
> into timber, white pine. (*The Back Country*, 20)

Noting the terrain in greater detail, the poet gives the reader an extremely concrete sense of life in this mountain wilderness; for the reader travels that rugged trail in his mind:

> gooseberry bush on the turns
> hooves clang on the riprap
> dust, brush, branches.
> a stone
> cairn at the pass —
> strippt mountains hundreds of miles.

In "Burning the Small Dead," Snyder feeds white pine into his campfire and watches the stars. With a few natural details, he conveys the simplicity and yet the profundity of this experience:

> a hundred summers
> snowmelt   rock   and air
>
> hiss in a twisted bough.
>
> sierra granite;
> Mt. Ritter —
> black rock twice as old.
>
> Deneb, Altair
>
> windy fire (*The Back Country*, 22)

In order to illustrate Rexroth's influence more specifically, it is necessary to discuss one other ingredient of this type of poetry. Although this characteristic of Rexroth's mountain poems does not appear in Snyder's work nearly as frequently, it is at times evident. In this respect, Rexroth's recent book on American poetry considers Snyder's vision to be essentially elegiac. Although there is truth in this pronouncement,[6] Rexroth's work seems to be more consistently elegiac than Snyder's. Much of Rexroth's back-country poetry is concerned with the death of a loved one, time wasted, or love lost; and good examples are his "Time Spirals" and his "Mocking Birds." In these poems, loneliness is mingled with the fond nostalgia of the Sung poets whom Rexroth reveres.

Certain of Snyder's nature poems approach this quality, and "For the Boy Who Was Dodger Point Lookout Fifteen Years Ago" is a good example of it. Originally published in *Holiday* as one of "Six Poems" (40, August, 1966), "For the Boy Who Was Dodger Point Lookout" was not included in the back-country section of Snyder's collected poems, A *Range of Poems*, published in March, 1966. It did, however, subsequently appear as the final poem in the first section, "Far West," of the completed version of *The Back Country* (1968). In the poem, Snyder returns to the location of an earlier back-packing trip he had taken with his first wife Alison Gass in the Olympic Mountains of Washington State. He describes the snow-melt pond in the grassy high country meadow, the Alpine vegetation and snowy peaks. Above the foaming creeks, he remembers, they lived as if suspended for a time in a "world of snow and flowers" (*The Back Country*, 34). Similarly, Rexroth, in his two elegies written for his dead wife Andree, states:

> My sorrow is so wide
> I cannot see across it;
> And so deep I shall never
> Reach the bottom of it.[7]

> Eighteen years
> Have passed since that autumn.
> There was no trail here then.[8]

As in "The Thin Edge of Your Pride: 1922–1926," where Rexroth writes for "You alone, A white robe over your naked body, / Passing and repassing / Through the dreams of twenty years" (36), and in "Climbing Milestone Mountain, August 22, 1937" where Rexroth retreats into the sanctity of the mountains, bitterly eulogizing Sacco and Vanzetti, Snyder addresses the lookout who had hiked down to visit him and his wife that day; and he concludes his poem with similar remorse and longing:

> I don't know where she is now;
> I never asked your name.
> In this burning, muddy, lying,
> blood-drenched world
> that quiet meeting in the mountains
> cool and gentle as the muzzles of
> three elk, helps keep me sane. (*The Back Country*, 34)

Although there are striking similarities between these two poems, it must be said that Rexroth and Snyder have totally different personalities. Consequently, Snyder's mountain poems generally lack the fatalism, the resignation and the haunted quality that are so pervasive in Rexroth's work. Snyder's Buddhism, spiritual buoyancy, pragmatic optimism, and sense of humor prevent this influence or presence. Although Rexroth was an early teacher, Snyder adapted the master's teachings to his own needs. Less psychically encumbered, thus stylistically less abstract and wordy, Snyder's nature poetry offers an immediacy, a lusty directness, which Rexroth's lacks. In short, Snyder's poems take the reader farther into the back country.

II   *"an extreme statement"*

While a forest-fire lookout on Sourdough Mountain in 1953, Snyder indicates in his journal, that he studied Chinese, did sumi painting, and read Blake and Thoreau (*Earth House Hold*, 12–24). Most important in this discussion, however, is his reading of Thoreau, since Snyder was then developing his concept of the wilderness which would provide the basis for much of his future work, especially *Mountains and Rivers Without End* and *The Back Country*. Although primarily responsive to the wilderness writing of Muir, Rexroth, and other Western Americans, Snyder did study *Walden* carefully during this formative period in his life, although as he has stated in a letter, he first read Thoreau at about age nineteen.[9] Certainly, even a cursory reading of Snyder's work reveals that the writings and the personal example of the hermit of Walden Pond were important to him.

When in 1862 Thoreau published "Walking," originally titled "The Wild" (in *Atlantic Monthly*), he wished to "speak a word for Nature, for absolute freedom and wildness, as contrasted with a freedom and culture merely civil, — to regard man as an inhabitant, or a part and parcel of Nature, rather than a member of society," and he added that he intended to make "an extreme statement." Since there were enough "champions of civilization,"[10] he became the first American to define the properties and to argue specifically the value and spiritual necessity of the wilderness. The earlier conception of wilderness (*wild-dēor*, Old Norse, "place of wild beasts") was negative; the first settlers on our American shores considered the wilderness as a place of danger and as the abode of the Devil. Thus came the rationale for cutting down the trees and letting in light, which Snyder explores in "Logging" in *Myths & Texts* (discussed in Chapter 4): "But ye shall destroy their altars, / break their images, and cut down their groves" (*Myths & Texts*, 4). On the other hand, a different response to wilderness developed in the late eighteenth and early nineteenth centuries, one that was later influenced by European Romanticism. The wilderness, as picturesque and sublime, was seen by the more refined and educated element of society as the locale of mystery and excitement, and often as the setting for religious experience. Early Deists, and later the Transcendentalists, with whom Thoreau was associated, enjoyed observing the wild scenery and considered its destruction as an act of desecration and sacrilege. Thus, the dichotomy between civilization and what was reverently called "Nature" occurred. In "For the West," Snyder expands upon this theme, likening Western civilization and "America" in particular to a "flowery glistening oil blossom / spreading on water. . . ." Continuting this metaphor Snyder presents its dangerous properties: "it was so tiny, nothing, now it keeps expanding. . ." (*The Back Country*, 103). When Thoreau spoke in *Walden* (1854) and later in "Walking," there were many who listened; for Thoreau was aware that a balance of civilization and wilderness was necessary for a healthy society: civilization was the source of culture and the arts; the wilderness, of strength, inspiration, and vigor. Thoreau believed that without a connection with wilderness, a people became weak and dull.

So great is and was the impact of the life and thought of Henry David Thoreau on Americans in general, and so similar are Thoreau and Snyder in many respects — philosophically, psychologically, and esthetically — that it is nearly impossible within the scope of this book to trace more than briefly the obvious points of comparison. Beyond an essentially individualistic, self-reliant, and aggressively creative approach to living, both Thoreau and Snyder exhibit a striking nonmaterialism by advocating economy and nonattachment — the "transcendent evenness of mind which enables one to participate in the temporal process without attachment,"[11] yet they uphold the absolute responsibility of maintaining an individual social conscience. Thoreau's "Essay on Civil Disobedience" and Snyder's "Buddhism and the Coming Revolution" indicate this attitude. As Snyder states in this essay, "No one today can afford to be innocent, or indulge himself in ignorance of the nature of contemporary governments, politics and social orders" (*Earth House Hold*, 90). This view, of course, is an emphatic expression of Thoreau's understanding of individual conscience. In addition, both Thoreau and Snyder are close and accurate observers of nature; and, although concerned with the macrocosm (both traveled and were students of the Orient), they are drawn inexorably toward the regions of their birth. These naturalistic and regionalistic tendencies are given expression in each writer's attempt to mythologize his own life and locale — Thoreau at Walden Pond, Snyder in the forests and mountains of the West. As a result, both developed new syntheses, or what might be considered new orientations to a life joyous, vigorous, and disciplined. This approach to life is described in Snyder's "How to Make Stew in the Pinacate Desert / Recipe For Locke & Drum." Snyder lustily describes in this poem, how this wilderness meal is methodically prepared with a mixture of store-bought and native ingredients. He then glories in its consumption: "and lift the black pot off the fire / to set aside another good ten minutes, / Dish it up and eat it with a spoon, sitting on a poncho in the dark" (*The Back Country*, 32).

As this poem indicates, the poetry of Snyder, like the works of Thoreau, is preeminently anti-Christian, even pagan. In this regard, both writers express profound respect for the American Indian and for nonhuman life forms; and they stress the importance of a knowledge of pre-history and of adherence to organic cycles rather than respond to formal institutions and dogma. The influence in particular on *Myths & Texts* of *Walden* which Snyder was reading while writing *Myths & Texts*, is evident in these respects. Following the example of Thoreau, Snyder makes his own life symbolic; he hatches a new myth in an attempt to raise consciousness and revitalize the society. The religious nature of the work, its organic and cyclic quality, its reverence for all life forms, and its essential cosmic optimism are seen in the last lines which quote the final sentence of *Walden*: "The sun is but a morning star" (*Myths & Texts*, 48). In summary, both Thoreau's and Snyder's determined search for authenticity prompted the necessity of living experimental lives. Thus, they take themselves and the world they live in seriously. In a sense, both seek to be heroes in their own place and time.

In 1965, before leaving for Japan, Snyder took a long backpacking trip to the Glacier Peak Wilderness Area of Washington State with poet Allen Ginsberg and a friend, Justine. At the summit of Glacier Peak, where only mountains are visible in all directions, Justine asked, "You mean there's a Senator for all this?" (*Earth House Hold*, 101). Snyder does not cite his answer in the journal; but, overcome by the view, he perhaps had none. However, more than five years later, in a statement delivered at a seminar at the Center for the Study of Democratic Institutions in Santa Barbara, California, Snyder gave his response which was subsequently published as "The Wilderness" in *New Directions in Prose and Poetry 23* and later collected in *Turtle Island*. Strikingly similar to the "extreme statement" made by Thoreau in "Walking" that advocates absolute freedom and wildness and is aware of man's place as an "inhabitant" of nature, Snyder relates and slightly reshapes the earlier Glacier Peak ascent and offers himself as the spokesman and the representative of the wilderness. Snyder writes, "Unfortunately, there isn't a senator for all that. And I would like to think of a new definition of humanism and a new definition of democracy that would include the nonhuman, that would have representation from those spheres."[12] Earlier in the speech Snyder states that "The reason I am here is because I wish to bring a voice from the wilderness, my constituency. I wish to be a spokesman for a realm that is not usually represented either in intellectual chambers or in the chambers of the government."[13]

Thoreau had associated the American West with the wild; and he had brought attention more than one hundred years before Snyder's speech to the problem of man's anthropocentrism and the consequent disenfranchisement of nature. As Snyder puts it, "At the root of the problem . . . is the mistaken belief that nature is something less authentic, that nature is not as alive as man is, or as intelligent, that in a sense it is dead. . . ."[14] Offering the American Indians' mythological consciousness and sensitivity to ecology as an example, Snyder's "The Wilderness," like "Walking," pleads its case with persistence. When the Pueblo Indians enacted their animal dances, "they were no longer speaking for humanity, they were taking it on themselves to interpret, through their humanity, what these other life forms were."[15] Thus, Snyder suggests that man consider the possibility of incorporating spokesmanship for the rest of life, for the wild, and that he thus create a truly democratic society.

Snyder conveys the life of seemingly inanimate nature and his mystical-ecological relationship to it in a poem, "By Frazier Creek Falls," recently collected in *Turtle Island*. More convincing than the speech at the Center in California, this poem involves the reader in the wilderness experience which Thoreau revered and wrote about throughout his life. Snyder, looking out and down from the edge of the falls, sees half-forested, dry hills and a clear sky, and he notices the effect of the wind in the pines, "rustling trembling limbs and twigs." The poet stands transfixed, listening. Ecstatically, he relates, "This living flowing land / is all there is, forever / We *are* it / it sings through us — ".[16] Similarly, Thoreau writes in "Walking" about the boundless joy he experienced while *sauntering* (trip to the "Holy Land" — *à la Sainte Terre*) in the wild. One gray November afternoon in particular, he relates, the sunlight broke through the clouds and "every wood and rising ground gleamed like the boundary of Elysium."[17]

III "The mountains are your mind"

Although Snyder's political and social views in regard to wilderness; his program for representation of the wild in a democratic society, based on the ideas of Thoreau; and the influence of Rexroth and the example his poetry offered for the utilization of wilderness as locale and theme have been discussed, more needs to be said about some of their interesting connections with Snyder's work:

first, between wilderness and the unconscious mind and their relationship to back-packing and meditation; second, and most importantly, between travel in backward ("third-world") countries and the
investigation of the demonic potential of the unconscious as exhibited in "Kali" in *The Back Country*. First Snyder's understanding
of the relationship between wilderness and the unconscious mind
should be discussed before tracing its use in "Kali" later in this
chapter.

Like Rexroth, Snyder became aware quite early in his career that
wilderness and the unconscious mind exhibit characteristics in
common: both seem remote and unknown, mysterious and enticing,
yet somehow forbidding. In a sense, both are "places" in which one
travels at one's own risk; therefore, one must have knowledge and
experience to enter them — be prepared or equipped. To Snyder,
the wilderness is the physical extension of the unconscious mind;
and, as a result, Snyder seemingly views the wilderness and the
mind as topographic and psychic territories to be explored. But not
only are they "fields of action"; more importantly, they are sources
of power or of personal energy — of a "power within" that is discussed in greater length later in this book.

In a very real way for Snyder, wilderness is a state of mind; in fact,
it is a condition of Snyder's own mind. In "the myth" which concludes *Myths & Texts*, Snyder writes that "The mountains are your
mind"; he does not state that they are *like* one's mind. Thus, wilderness for Snyder, it would seem, is not only synonymous with "wild
mind," the unconscious, but it mystically becomes, or *is*, "wild
mind." Not only does wilderness represent the freedom and untap-
ped possibilities of the unconscious, not only is it a locale to which
one can escape and gain the insight, or even the ecstasy, often
obtained in solitude; wilderness is what the poet Robert Bly has
called the "landscape of the imagination."[18] As Bly suggests, the
imagination, or "mind" of Snyder and other Western American
writers, differs from that of the Eastern urban writer. Snyder thinks
imaginatively, rather than rhetorically; that is, he understands in
the "forms of the imagination rather than in the forms of abstraction. . . ."[19] In short, in Snyder's thought, geography and psychology blend. The poet's trip through the wilderness and through the
"backward" countries of the world, although used artistically as
metaphor, even allegory, becomes on another level not only the
tracing of the psychic maze but the maze itself. As Snyder quotes in

the broadside "Four Changes," " 'Wildness is the state of complete awareness'."

As should be evident, Snyder's perception of wilderness goes beyond that of Thoreau and Rexroth. Because Snyder is a Buddhist, his perception is essentially mystical and pre-scientific. Moreover, Snyder's response to wilderness is self-reflexive: he makes personal use of nature, and he never studies it apart from himself. To the Buddhist, all is unified in what is called "One Mind." Although men may live on different levels of that totality, they are all part of a great oneness. Thus, when Snyder states that wilderness is an extension of mind, he does not mean that it is, therefore, separate from it. Such misunderstanding is caused by the inadequacy of language, rather than by the condition itself. Certainly, there is much truth in the Buddhist notion that all is mind, for men only know what their senses perceive and their brains decode. Linguists also point out that, in a real way, everyone lives in his mind.

In this regard, Thomas Parkinson points out that Snyder's aim is "not to achieve harmony with nature but to create an inner human harmony. . . ." This relationship, Parkinson states, is not an "allegorical relation" but an "analogical one. . . ."[20] The poet establishes within himself a state of being which is equivalent to that of nature. Snyder's relationship to nature is, perhaps, essentially epistemological; that is, to Snyder, life and insight are one; consciousness is existence; and ultimately the universal is the particular. In discussing Thoreau, Sherman Paul has indicated that the poet becomes "the link between the actual and the ideal." Since he shapes his life by the idea that he has in his mind, he seeks what Paul calls a "conquest by consciousness," which is "that perfect oneness or relatedness to the universe that comes from the assimilation of the world by the mind. . . ."[21]

In view of what has been stated above, one can understand Snyder's interest in back-packing and in meditation. His concern is, of course, with methodology because both are modes of "travel" and because both provide access to this psychic territory. *Zazen,* or more specifically *kinhin* (walking meditation), is a kind of meditational back-packing in which one goes as far as one can on as little as possible. Snyder is so aware of the need to search for and come to terms with one's unconscious mind, with this wild territory, in order to become liberated and happy that he has written "Buddhism and the Coming Revolution." In this article, Snyder uses the term "revolution" to mean change of consciousness. He mentions that the achievement of Buddhism has been the development of a practical system of meditation. This practice, a matter of action and not of belief, "for which one needs only 'the ground beneath one's feet'," Snyder relates, "wipes out mountains of junk being pumped into the mind by the mass media and supermarket universities" (*Earth House Hold*, 91). Earlier in *A Controversy of Poets* Snyder had stated this same idea, but in a different way: "There's not much wilderness left to destroy, and the nature in the mind is being logged and burned off."[22] "Buddhism and the Coming Revolution" concludes with the suggestion that "whatever is or ever was in any other culture can be reconstructed from the unconscious, through meditation" (93).

IV "Kali"

Although *The Back Country* was published in 1968, many of the poems were written considerably earlier during a period of remorse, frustration, and uncertainty. Such poems are concerned with Snyder's quest to define himself or, as he states, to do "what my / karma demands" (*The Back Country*, 47). In *The Back Country*, the trials and tribulations, the pain and exaltation of his psychic journey, his quest for sanity and wholeness, are recorded. In this rambling work, which is less formally unified than *Myths & Texts* and which is more similar to *Mountains and Rivers Without End*, Snyder's spiritual vagrancy unfolds. In "I Far West," Snyder rambles through the mountains and along the rivers of the American West like Bashō, the Zen poet whom Snyder quotes on his dedication page as "roaming, roving the coast up and / down. . . ." As Snyder wanders through Japan in "II Far East," he learns to meditate and studies Zen in an attempt to know himself better. And, in "IV Back," he returns to this country.

Most interesting for the reader in the context of this discussion, however, is his trip to India in 1962 that is preserved in the poems collected in "III Kali." Snyder, who seems very near to the reader, reveals more in these poems of early manhood than elsewhere. One not only experiences his "dark night of the soul" and sees him struggle with doubt and uncertainty but also witnesses the terror, the failure, and the gradual, but ultimate enlightenment and fulfillment in "IV Back." Not only is India the field and the catalyst for

Snyder's struggle and ultimate insight, but it is also another kind of back country or "backward" country. Whereas the American wilderness both represents and, as mentioned above, is for Snyder all that is positive and life-affirming in the unconscious, India seems to manifest what is negative, or demonic; and one follows Snyder into hell in "Kali".

India deeply impressed Snyder because, as he has written, its philosophies and mythologies were "vast, touching the deepest areas of the mind . . ." (*Earth House Hold*, 114). More directly, the physical impact of the Indian experience seems to have been overpowering. The rawness of India, the absolute poverty, the crush of humanity and the lack of privacy, the self-effacement in conjunction with extreme arrogance, and the close proximity of passivity and violence coalesced to create for Snyder a picture of life laid bare. In "Journey to Rishikesh and Hardwar," Snyder relates an incident which may have inspired sections of "The Market" in *Mountains and Rivers Without End*. Leaving Rishikesh, Snyder and his fellow travelers buy a quart of curds, make a "monster fruit-and-curds salad," and please "secret hungers . . ." (*Earth House Hold*, 88). More typical of their experiences, however, is Section III of "The Market" which offers a vivid picture of the more terrifying aspects of life in India:

> they eat feces
> > in the dark
> > on stone floors.
> > one legged animals, hopping cows
> > limping dogs   blind cats
>
> crunching garbage in the market
> > broken fingers
> > > cabbage
> > head on the ground.
>
> who has young face.
> > open pit eyes
> between the bullock carts and people
> > head pivot with the footsteps
> > > > passing by
> dark scrotum spilld on the street
> > penis laid by his thigh
> > > torso
> turns with the sun[23]

In this poem the reader senses the rawness of human existence. Although understated, Snyder's horror, even revulsion, is clear as he paints a terrifying picture of suffering, inhumanity, and human debasement. Its starkness and its suppressed violence are overpowering. The images of animals eating excrement in the dark off stone floors is extremely unnerving. Cold and darkness are archetypal experiences all men fear. The image is developed; its effect intensified; for the reader hears garbage crunched, sees a "young face" with "open pit eyes" . . . "pivot with the footsteps" . . . "dark scrotum spilld upon the street / penis laid by his thigh. . . ." In response to the overpowering experience of such suffering, the poet concludes the poem by stating that he only "came to buy / a few bananas by the ganges / while waiting for my wife" (37).

Although Snyder presents this dark side of India in "The Market," as a horrific and terrible hell on earth, another side of India is presented that is boundless in acceptance of life, fertile and overtly sexual. This side is, in the main, only a glimmer of the pre-Moslem India when statuary and frieze-work depicted scantily clad women with moon-shaped breasts, when a type of sexual yoga in which intercourse became prayer was practiced, and when the *Kama-sutra* was written. In *Earth House Hold*, Snyder writes of Indian eroticism as "hips and breasts, agile limbs on stone floors with intricate design" (40). The "Kali" poems from *The Back Country* present a more complete picture in this respect, although the dark aspects are stressed. In "For a Stone Girl at Sanchi," Snyder describes this ancient art work:

> loving;
> two flesh persons changing,
>   clung to, door frames
>   notions, spear-hafts
> in a rubble of years. (*The Back Country*, 68)

The "Kali" poems, as Snyder states on the flyleaf of *The Back Country*, were, as mentioned above, inspired by his visit to India and by his reading of Indian religious texts, "particularly those of Shaivism and Tibetan Buddhism. . . ." Kali, the goddess of death, the destroyer, in Indian mythology, is usually depicted as black in color; and since she is the earth-mother, she is associated with dark, obscene rites. In Western terms, Kali might represent the demonic or, more specifically, the fearful aspects of the unconscious mind. Although the contrast between the angelic and demonic is developed in these poems, as we have seen, Snyder essentially associates the demonic with his Indian experience and with Indian culture. Snyder apparently had an experience in India he had not expected that so jolted his unconscious that it dredged up feelings and images he had not known were there. India's lack of control and discipline unnerved Snyder. In "Now, India," he writes "The POINT is, though, from my standpoint, that there was no practice of any kind . . . & this is what I am always looking for."[24]

Clearly, India was psychically as well as physically threatening to Snyder. The respect he learned for Indian culture and the delicate balance of terror and delight, pain and joy, which he experienced as expressed in the Indian concept of *maya*, are evident. At the conclusion of "Now, India" Snyder writes: "Now we are about to leave India, and feeling very lucky to have come through it all intact. . . . And glad to be leaving, then, because India is not comfortable." However, although aware of the "Dishonesty, cheating, hostility, rudeness, loudness, thoughtlessness . . . ," which frequently aroused his temper, Snyder had to admit that there is a "kind of honesty in India which is ultimately lacking in Japan. . . ." He concludes, "In the end India was most impressive to me because of a deep feeling of substantiality & solidness it has."[25]

Certainly, India in her art, religion, and culture has explored thoroughly the unconscious life of man. Taking the suggestion of the Orient, Snyder relates in *Earth House Hold* the necessity of self-analysis for psychic wholeness: ". . . it is necessary to look exhaustively into the negative and demonic potentials of the Unconscious, and by recognizing these powers — symbolically acting them out — one releases himself from these forces" (*Earth House Hold*, 115). Possibly, this is the way in which the journey to India and the poems inspired by it functioned for Snyder. The poems might be seen as a record of a Dantean journey to the underworld of the mind. The "shock of recognition" Snyder apparently experienced during those six months in India and the manifestations of the demonic he saw expressed visibly in the streets — the chaos, the lust, the anger, the hostility — caused him to realize that these qualities existed also in him. The exploration of India and of other "backward" countries was, therefore, the outward extension of his journey into his own mind. As well as providing the stage, India

dramatized that psychic journey; for it is significant that the final
section of *The Back Country* is entitled "Back."

"Kali" begins with a description of the goddess (who is hereafter
refered to as the demonic) as fearful, black, and naked; and Snyder's
ink drawing beneath this description evokes the sense of a gaping
pudendum. In Kali, who symbolizes the human capacities and
needs men are ashamed of and fear, Indian culture demonstrated to
Snyder the need to face these facts of human existence and to come
to terms with his own negative potential. In "Kali," Snyder descends into the world of spirits, explores this realm, and acknowledges its condition. He ritualizes his awareness. Symbolically acting
out his fears and lusts in his poems, he exorcizes their effect on him,
and finally achieves liberation and harmony.

Snyder prefaces "Kali" with a short Amerindian song:

> When I went down
> to sea-lion town
> my wife was dead
> the canoes were gone *(The Back Country,* 66)

Thus, Snyder begins his psychic trip into the place of chaos and
develops the themes of death and lost love which run through
"Kali." This section also offers a number of poems concerning unhappy love affairs, an unsuccessful marriage, and incidents of un-
satisfactory relationships with women. In "Alysoun," the poet
writes, "You whimpered all night long / with evil dreams / in a toss-
ing bed by me . . ." (67). In "To Hell with Your Fertility Cult,"
which depicts a marital argument, the woman hits the man with an
egg: " — he had nothing to say" (67). In "Robin," the poet remembers his wife with longing and remorse: they have parted, and he
misses her. In "Kali," the hell of drunkenness is also explored when
Snyder describes his stupor in "A Dry Day Just Before the Rainy
Season" and asks, "I wonder what I said to everybody" (72).

In "Kali," Snyder also unearths and displays the depths of human
degradation. In "Mother of the Buddhas" Snyder shows an "old sow
in the mud," "deep in food dirt," "her warm filth, / deep-plowing
snout, / dragging teats" (83). The intensified sense of death, decay,
and dirt that are so prevalent and obvious in India is related in
"Wandering the Old, Dirty Countries":

> Well   yes   malnutrition
> Bad teeth, shit-stained babies
> Flies around the eyes,
>
>   . . .
> Bustards   loosefeathered
> Vultures hunched on hills (84)

This sense of human carrion is continued in "Circumnambulating Arunachala." In one particular image, selected while circling this holy mountain, Snyder describes

> Small girls with gaudy flowers
> flash down the bare walk road,
>   the weight, the power,
>   the full warm brilliance of the human mind
>   behind their eyes:
>   they die or sicken in a year. (86)

In "On Our Way to Khajuraho," he offers a glimpse of the effects of the caste system: "On our way to / Khajuraho / . . . a girl thirteen / gave us pice in change / . . . she must have been low caste. / the girl stood off . . ." (84–85). As if in response to circumstances such as these which repress creativity, deny human potential, and create such negative effect, Snyder expresses the sense of time wasted and energies lost that he saw in India in poems such as "The Truth Like the Belly of a Woman Turning":

> who
> cares.
>   CRYING
> all these passt,
>   losst,
>   years. (89).

In "Maya," written for the poet Peter Orlovsky, Snyder explores the pleasures and dangers of drugs. As the title indicates, these pleasures bring delight and temporary escape from suffering. But similar to other earthly pleasures, they enslave or, in Hindu terms, keep man "on the wheel of birth and death." More profound, however, is the despair and desolation Snyder first experienced while a student of Zen in Japan. "This Tokyo" reveals the "Hopelessness where love of man / Or hate of man could matter / None . . . ." Snyder states, "love . . . / Contemplate . . . / But know . . . / that all you tread / Is earthquake rot and matter mental / Trembling. . ." (*The Back Country*, 74–75). In this poem Snyder's awareness of man's utter helplessness is clear and it is terrifying to realize that men are alone with no props and are dependent "On the meeting of sun and earth. . ." (74). A similar sentiment is expressed in another Snyder poem, "A Stone Garden," published in an earlier collection but written about the same time, in which Snyder states,

> And I that night prowled Tokyo like a bear
> Tracking the human future
> Of intelligence and despair. (*Riprap*, 21–22)

In these two poems, Snyder expresses his realization of the "existential emptiness" for mankind of our time and he suggests that men must face this fact if they are to live truthfully and achieve "transcendent fullness." Although "This Tokyo" was written prior to his trip to India, it is appropriately included in the "Kali" section because of its theme. In this poem, Snyder writes in ultimate terms, abjures immediate social and personal goals and makes a strongly existential statement. Snyder also presents his realization that fragile and weak man is relatively unimportant in nature; his existence is tentative. Lost in a self-created world of symbols, men are not certain what is real and what is illusion. However, man is morally free; he can do what he wishes. This realization, or *kensho* as the Buddhists call it, is overpowering in the liberation it brings; but the loneliness that results, which the reader feels in this poem, is overpowering.

This sense of the transience of life, of the immutability of change, and of man's consequent mortality is also evoked in "What Do They Say" in which the reader feels the unhappiness which aging can affect. Here are images of absence, the unhappy response to change, and the consequent isolation, loneliness, and inability to communicate one's feelings. The reader sees the "for sale" sign, soot on the window sill, a garden full of weeds; and he remembers

> The glimpse of once-loved face
>   gone into a train.
> Lost in a new town, no one knows the name.

>   lone man sitting in the park
>   Chanced on by a friend
>   of thirty years before. . . . (*The Back Country*, 81)

In "Looking At Pictures To Be Put Away," the poet asks,

>   What will we remember
>   Bodies thick with food and lovers
>   After twenty years. (*The Back Country*, 89)

In other poems in "Kali," Snyder develops further the theme of human mortality and insignificance. In "The Manichaeans," he writes that his body and that of the woman he loves, when burned, make "eight pounds of / Pure white mineral ash." He also presents man as a continually evolving being: "as you rest with your chin back / your arms are still flippers / your lidded eyes lift from a swamp. . . ." And, when Snyder relates the sense of human existence to love-making, he concludes that, if the universe is so vast and if life so short, "Let us touch — for if two lie together / Then they have warmth. / We shall sink in this heat / of our arms / . . . And keep back the cold" (76–77). This practical and realistic poem satisfies the reader on a humanistic level more than does the cold realism of "This Tokyo." Contrary to the dictates of the third-century A.D. Persian named Mani, who believed that the denial of sensual pleasure would be rewarded by immediate happiness after death, Snyder ironically entitles his poem "The Manichaeans," for he advocates the efficacy of love-making and suggests that it is all we have. And, even though there are no ultimate answers ("peace, war, religion, revolution, will not help"), to make love is enjoyable and practical. Snyder also suggests that man cannot deal anyway with absolutes: ". . . the agile / Thumb and greedy little brain . . ." is limited. Men may be "worthless / To each other . . ." ("This Tokyo"); but, as this poem suggests, there is much they can do for each other. We can love, at least temporarily, and with deep satisfaction.

Further development of the theme of living fully, despite the existence of the void, is seen in "Xrist." In this poem Snyder rejects the idea of human sacrifice by dramatizing the concept in terms of the many mythic figures who have initiated, or symbolized, human sacrifice of one kind or another. Snyder sees all these figures and the cults which followed them as manifestations of the same drive or

psychological need. Christ, Snyder regards as the greatest trans-
gressor: he sacrificed himself and suggested that all others do so.
Since Snyder cannot understand this kind of thinking, he returns to
an affirmation of the senses; indeed, abstract statements are usually
followed by references to specific objects in Snyder's poems. Typically, the poetic rendering of the Indian corn-woman myth in
"Could She See the Whole Real World With Her Ghost Breast Eyes
Shut Under a Blouse Lid" ends with the matter-of-fact statement
that " 'Once a bear gets hooked on garbage there's no cure' " (The
Back Country, 70). There are no saviors, according to Snyder.

With this awareness of the need to live fully, Snyder does not
accept the need for sacrifice and self-immolation; and, as a result,
images of self-destruction and sacrifice drawn from many diverse
cultures fill the poem. He describes self-immolation in Athens, the
sacrificed virgin in Central America, and the primitive puberty rites
that involve mutilation. All these practices, suffered for a greater
good, not only offend Snyder's sense of humanity but contradict his
view of reality. What Christianity calls the Devil is to Snyder the
unrestrained powers of nature, both external and internal; and these
anarchic forces are deeply feared by the socially stratified and ordering powers of organized religion. Specifically, the unconscious force
of lust was mythologized quite early as the Devil. To desire profoundly, deeply, or compulsively was to be under the power of the
Devil. This concept was a convenient way to externalize and give
visible shape to what is inside one, and thus exorcize and pass on the
guilt feelings to another.

In commenting on the Judeo-Christian tradition and the association of the Devil with unrestrained nature, Snyder relates: "The
Devil? 'The Deivill apeired vnto her in the likenes of ane prettie boy
in grein clothes. . . .' 'He wold haw carnall dealling with ws in the
shap of a deir, or in any vther shap, now and then, somtyme he vold
be lyk a stirk, a bull, a deir, a rae, or a dowg, etc, and haw dealling
with us' " (Earth House Hold, 122). It is interesting to note that in
this passage the demonic, in this case human lust, is associated with
the color green and with nature and animals in particular. Nature,
or the devil, is thought to be dangerous; but in reality, as the poem
indicates, nature is wise and immutable: "The bruised snake coils in
the grass" (79). Christianity mythologizes the demonic as a snake,
and the snake, like a free-flowing penis, a symbol of sexuality, has
been feared and hated. However, when nature is not seen as de-

monic, the snake becomes an appropriate symbol of the pervasi~~
and immutable powers of nature which are not propitiated or altered, much less controlled, by man and his religious practices.

In summary, the poems in "Kali," especially the three discussed
in detail, display significant aspects of Snyder's world view and trace
his journey through the dark maze of his own unconscious mind in
his quest for wisdom. "This Tokyo" presents Snyder's existentialism;
"The Manichaeans," his reverence for life and sensuous delight; and
"Xrist," his rejection of sacrifice as undisciplined and cruel, as inef-
fectual and inconsequential. Dramatized in terms of his travels in
"backward countries," Snyder's psychic descent into the unconscious lays bare the many facets of the demonic as exhibited in
human behavior; and the reader sees all manner of activity and is
shocked and disheartened. Out of this struggle with psychic demons, however, the poet returns whole with a liberating awareness
of the demonic in himself and of his place in the endless process of
energy transformation. As expressed in "Go Round" and "[After
Rāmprāsad Sen]" and to be explored further in *Regarding Wave*,
Snyder can "Now . . . turn to the hunt," as he relates in one of the
final poems in "Kali"; and he can do so with "Blade sharp and hair on
end / over the boulders / eager / tasting the snow" (*The Back Country*, 92).

CHAPTER 7

Regarding the Energy

SIGNIFICANTLY influenced by specific American scientific works such as John Holdren and Philip Herrera's *energy*, and *Energy and Power*, a Scientific American anthology, Snyder's interests have shifted recently from social science to pure science. In *Regarding Wave* and *Turtle Island*, science not only functions as "corroboration" for what Snyder has been saying since *Myths & Texts*, but also serves in a highly personalized way as a "gloss" or as a frame of reference. Specifically, Snyder's interest in science has centered on the subject of energy; for Snyder would agree with Freeman J. Dyson's statement in "Energy in the Universe" that "We do not know how the scientists of the next century will define energy or in what strange jargon they will discuss it. But no matter what language the physicists use they will not come into contradiction with Blake. Energy will remain in some sense the lord and giver of life, a reality transcending our mathematical descriptions. Its nature lies at the heart of the mystery of our existence as animate beings in an inanimate universe.[1] The themes of Snyder's early career — the beauty and purposiveness of animals, the mysteriousness, grace and quiet power of women ("Praise for Sick Women"), the wilderness as physical extension of the unconscious mind (*The Back Country*), and man's undeniable and strategic position in the food web (*Myths & Texts*) — coalesce in his present fascination with energy and the quest for spiritual power as presented in *Regarding Wave*. Quoting from William Blake's "The Marriage of Heaven and Hell" (1793), Snyder has entitled a recent article first published in The *New York Times*, and later collected in *Turtle Island*, " 'Energy is Eternal Delight'."[2] This essay expresses Snyder's mystical belief in the existence of the "true" energy in man, manifested as "the power within."

An early reference to the quest for spiritual energy is found in "Note on Religious Tendencies," published in June, 1959, in which Snyder states that "Vision and illumination seeking" is pre-eminent with the Beat Generation. In this statement, he stresses the importance of discipline and method in attaining spiritual energy and cites as examples the great wisdom traditions of the "Quakers, Shinshu, Buddhism, Sufism."[3] In *Riprap*, published in the same year, Snyder explores the locale of his birth and early manhood. *Myths & Texts* (1960), a more concentrated and scholarly work that is peopled with all types of beautiful plants and animals, mythologizes their lives and creates the context for Snyder's treatment of energy in later works. *Mountains and Rivers Without End* (1965) records the poet's quest of himself and America. One section in particular, "The Market," catalogues Snyder's purchases at various exotic markets and establishes, as Thomas Parkinson has written, "equivalences of energy. . . ."[4] A more recent section of *Mountain and Rivers Without End*, "The Blue Sky" (1969), deals with Amerindian psycho-medicine and the magical use of language for healing. *The Back Country* (1968) presents Snyder's belief that the wilderness is the physical extension of the unconscious mind and that both are sources of unlimited spiritual energy. And "Poetry and the Primitive," the central essay in *Earth House Hold* (1969), explores the nature of poetry as access, — as a vehicle of liberation. So intimate is the relationship between poetry and energy that Snyder considers it an "Ecological Survival Technique" (117). Indeed, Snyder's response to poetry is similar to his use of Zen meditation as a source of spiritual energy. His belief — influenced by his Buddhist studies where he found that voice is an expression of body, speech, and mind, and is, therefore, a manifestation of god's creative energy — is given poetic expression in *Regarding Wave* (1970). In *Earth House Hold*, he writes that "Poetry is the vehicle of the mystery of voice. The universe . . . is a vast breathing body" (118). Later, he adds that "Poetry is voice, and according to Indian Tradition, voice, vāk, (vox) — is a Goddess" (124). "As Vāk is wife to Brahma ['wife,' according to Snyder, means 'wave' means 'vibrator' in Indo-European etymology] so the voice, in everyone, is a mirror of his own deepest self. The voice rises to answer an inner need . . ." (125). In this respect, *Turtle Island* (1974) offers Snyder's most recent poetic statement concerning energy. More abstract and explicitly scientific in nature, *Turtle Island* develops many of the themes which cluster around the quest for alternate sources of energy.

One other point of introduction should be made because Snyder uses the term "energy" in a different sense than do the politician or the businessman. In "Mother Earth," published in The *New York Times*, and collected as "Mother Earth: Her Whales" in enlarged form in *Turtle Island*, Snyder asks, "How can the . . . bureaucrats / Speak for the green of the leaf? Speak for the soil? / Speak for man?"[5] In response to his own question, he suggests that men learn the energy "network" of their own immediate environments and find true growth within themselves. In "Oil," he had already written (*The Back Country*, 26) of the "crazed, hooked nations" that are dependent upon outside sources of fossil fuel for energy, and he reiterates this point in " 'Energy is Eternal Delight'." As Snyder expresses his view in this article, "The longing for growth is not wrong. The nub of the problem now is how to flip over, as in *jujitsu*, the magnificent growth-energy of modern civilization into a nonacquisitive search for deeper knowledge of self and nature." Snyder concludes, "Electricity for Los Angeles is not energy."[6]

Translating science into poetry, Snyder points in the direction of William Blake. As Blake expresses this condition in "The Marriage of Heaven and Hell," "2. Energy is the only life, and is from / the Body; and Reason is the bound or / outward circumference of Energy. / 3. Energy is Eternal Delight."[7] To Blake and Snyder "real" energy emanates from internal sources and is not given; for such real energy is spiritual power, the "power within." Snyder displays this realization in a recent poem, "Without," in which he suggests we look for

the silence
of nature
within.

the power within.
the power

without.
. . .

singing

the proof

the proof of the power within. (*Turtle Island*, 6)

I *"The movements of the triad of mother, father and child"*

On the flyleaf of *Regarding Wave*, the editors quote Snyder: "The title, *Regarding Wave* reflects 'a half-buried series of word origins dating back through the Indo-European language: intersections of energy, woman, song and 'Gone Beyond Wisdom'." As Snyder has stated, and as his editors repeat, he holds " ' the most archaic values on earth'." In *Regarding Wave*, these basic principles which are first explored at length in *Myths & Texts* reach synthesis in "energy," the power within. In "Wave," the lead poem, Snyder regards the energy in the universe, and he observes its infinite number of frozen manifestations as waves. He regards the

> Grooving clam shell,
>   streakt through marble,
>   sweeping down ponderosa pine bark-scale
>   rip-cut tree grain
>   sand-dunes, lava
>   flow (*Regarding Wave*, 13)

He observes another energy manifestation, his own mind:

> Ah, trembling spreading radiating wyf
>   racing zebra
> catch me and fling me wide
> To the dancing grain of things
>   of my mind! (3)

In *Regarding Wave*, energy manifestations — or fields such as mind (consciousness), language (voice), and food (meat and plants) — combine and are given expression in terms of Snyder's domestic situation that is made symbolic. To Snyder, the family is an energy network. In a poem written after the publication of *Regarding Wave*, "Prayer for the Great Family," Snyder offers gratitude to all the sources of energy — the earth, plants, air, animals, water, the sun. In part, he expresses:

> Gratitude to Mother Earth, sailing through night and day —
> and to her soil: rich, rare, and sweet
> *in our minds so be it.* (*Turtle Island*, 24)

Of particular importance as a source of energy, as this "Prayer" indicates, is the figure of the mother or of the woman as wife, described in "Wave" as " 'veiled; vibrating; vague' " (*Regarding Wave*,3), that is, as mysterious and profound. Also in "No Matter, Never Mind," Snyder links the wife with energy and ultimately with mind:

> The Father is the Void
> The Wife   Waves
>
> Their child is Matter.
>
> Matter makes it with his mother
> And their child is Life,
>   a daughter.
>
> The Daughter is the Great Mother
> Who, with her father / brother Matter
>   as her lover,
>
> Gives birth to the Mind. (*Turtle Island*, 11)

In *Regarding Wave* in particular, Snyder's wife, Masa, to whom this cycle of poems is dedicated, becomes the primary physical manifestation of energy in the universe: she is the voice, the vibrator, the energy-giver, and the "goddess" who represents the energy within mankind's deepest selves. As Snyder states in "Regarding Wave," relating poetry to the feminine principle or muse, "The Voice / is a wife / to / him still" (*Regarding Wave*, 35). Thus, woman becomes the "voice within us" which is given form in the symbol of "The Great Mother" of *Turtle Island*, the Paleolithic fertility goddess of the mother cult, represented in the voluptuous, sculptured stone figures such as the "Venus of Willendorf," thought by Robert Graves to be the source of all poetry.[8]

Snyder's most recent marriage has definitely altered the pattern of his life. After the wedding ceremony, celebrated in the summer of 1967 on the edge of the crater of an active volcano on Suwa-No-Se Island, Snyder with his wife, Masa, returned to the United States; and the satisfaction which his present marriage has brought to

Snyder is evident. More specifically, the birth of his first son, Kai, the following year has had a profound impact on Snyder. Kai himself; Snyder's experience of watching the birth with old Mrs. Tanaka the midwife officiating; Kai's passing through the interface between this world and that of the womb—all these greatly energized the poet. Earlier in "[After Rāmprāsad Sen]," Snyder had written of birth and rebirth: "Arms shielding my face / Knees drawn up / Falling through flicker / Of womb after womb . . ." (*The Back Country*, 94); but he had sired no offspring until 1968. At thirty-eight, Snyder was ready for fatherhood; and the birth and everything which surrounded it produced an epiphany in Snyder. In Thomas Parkinson's words, this birth was the "moment that changes all being."[9] Consequently, Snyder completed his formal Zen studies, returned to the United States and re-established connections with this society, entered into dedicated teaching and aggressive eco-activism, ultimately built his own home in the Sierras, and experimented with new forms of familial structure.

Especially interesting in this respect is the central grouping of poems in *Regarding Wave* that concern the birth of Snyder's first son that are entitled "It Was When," "The Bed in the Sky," "Kai, Today," and "Not Leaving the House." In the first poem, "It Was When," the poet attempts to determine where his son was conceived. Was it in the bamboo house, on a jungle ridge by a snag, in the farmhouse at night, or on the boulders at south beach? At that moment, Snyder writes, the "blood of the moon stoppt" (*Regarding Wave*, 31); and Masa was released from the limitations of menstruation that are related in "Praise for Sick Women" (*Riprap*). The procreative act not only liberates her but causes energy, the "waves," to flow into her. The seed takes its place in her womb, and a "new power in [her] breath called its place" (31). As a result, she exhibits "the grace" which comes with spiritual power.

In "Kai, Today," however, Snyder presents even more baffling questions. Reverently, and in awe, he asks, how did it occur? Where did this being to be called "Kai" come from? What was his previous existence? In this respect, Snyder relates the paradoxical Zen *koan*, "What's your from-the-beginning face?" That is, what did you look like before your mother and father were born? This *koan* shows the limitations of logical thinking as a means of understanding the mystery of birth and death over which man has puzzled for forty thousand years. Plato's view as transmitted by Wordsworth and other Romantic poets, states that one existed somewhere before birth. To Plato, that existence was somehow more perfect, more intense; and, as Wordsworth wrote in "Ode: Intimations of Immortality from Recollections of Early Childhood," of that earlier, pristine state, birth is but a forgetting. To Wordsworth:

> The Soul that rises with us, our life's Star,
> Hath had elsewhere its setting,
> And cometh from afar:
> Not in entire forgetfulness,
> And not in utter nakedness,
> But trailing clouds of glory do we come
> From God, who is our home. . . .[10]

Snyder poked fun at these lines in his matter-of-fact way in "Go Round": "we enter this world trailing / slippery clouds of guts / incense of our flowery flesh" (*The Back Country*, 93). To Snyder, a Buddhist, birth is not "a forgetting" but a transformation, as he relates in "Hunting, 10," *Myths & Texts:* "Flung from demonic wombs / off to some new birth / A million shapes . . ." (27).

To Snyder these transformations are not so easily understood or so simply explained as Plato and Wordsworth suggest. Nonetheless, Snyder pursues this troubling matter in "Kai, Today." He relates early memories of himself and of Masa before they met: he was stretching by the river; she, scared by a beggar in the tough shipping section of Tokyo, was weeping and seeking safety in the arms of her elder sister. Snyder searches these memories in an effort to make sense of them. As Snyder implies, their meeting was somehow fated ("these fates"). He speculates, how he, a Northwestern American, and Masa, a Japanese, had come together. What impelled Snyder to travel to Japan, ultimately meet Masa, marry, and procreate? What conjunction of forces, or fields of energy, were in effect? And Why?

The actual birth of Kai, as related in "Kai, Today," further probes the unfathomable nature of birth. Before reading this poem in public, Snyder usually explains that, while he observed the birth of

> Kai.
> born again
> To the Mother's hoarse bear-down
> groan and dark red mask:

> spiralling, glistening, blue-white, up
>
> And out from her [,]

he had a vision, remembered from his days as a sailor on an oil
tanker in the Persian Gulf, of

> dolphins leaping in threes
> through blinding inter-
> faces. . . . (*Regarding Wave*, 33)

Because of some deeper level of consciousness of the reader, a
strong connection exists between birth and the dolphins who leap
up and out of the wave-slip of the ship. The interface, the surface
which forms a common boundary between two bodies, the sea as
Great Mother, source of all life; the wave-slip a vast vagina, "opening, boundless"; the dolphins, "leaping," "arching" like children,
the *"whap"* as they hit the water like the slap on the buttocks of a
newborn baby — all these details, both recently observed and remembered, come together to effect a profound response on a level
deeper than that of the logical mind.

In "The Bed in the Sky," a poem which evokes the sense of a
supernatural marriage, Snyder rides home on his motorcycle at
night to enter the bed, which is described in feminine terms as "full
and spread and dark." He embraces his wife, sinks "into the warm"
(*Regarding Wave*, 32); and, his stomach against her belly, "feels
[their] baby turn." Snyder's joy concerning the growth of the fetus,
the development of his child, is obvious. In addition, his new sense
of responsibility and purpose is also evident; for, when he would
like "to stay outside alone / and watch the moon all night," his
growing sense of paternity and of the dependency of his family on
his health and safety restrain him. He weaves "a safe path through"
icy streets. The poet's maturity and new response to mortality ("The
cemetery behind / Namu Amida Butsu / chiselled ten thousand
times") are mirrored in the orderliness and classic purity of the
poem. Snyder rarely employs rhyme; yet in "The Bed in the Sky"
end rhyme is used with discretion and to good effect ("white" rhyming with "night"). The meter in stanza four is essentially iambic
trimeter with a four-stress variation, simple and basic, nearly perfect in symmetry, and quite effective in intensifying the sense of
purpose and discipline felt by the poet at this time:

Tires crackle the mud-puddles
The northern hills gleam white
    I ought to stay outside   alone
        and watch the moon all night *(Regarding Wave,* 32)

The last line of the poem, significantly short, is set off from the preceding five stanzas and produces a characteristically strong response in the reader. In addition, the line "feels our baby turn" ends on a consonant. The "rn" sound is a nasal. The vowel sound preceding it is soft. The total effect, which continues on and is not stopped, is warm and soft, essentially feminine, and consistent, therefore, with the subject of the poem.

This sense of familial love and unity is movingly portrayed in "Not Leaving the House," the last poem in this birth sequence. In this poem, the poet "quit[s] going out"; he hangs around the house and watches his wife and son intently. Everything seems so new and so special that even simple tasks, such as washing, sleeping, baking bread, or drinking tea, assume a sacramental significance. This sense of ritual is intensified by the poet's listing of the objects brought for his son and placed ceremoniously around the bed: Navajo beads, peacock tail feather, badger pelt, and a pot of yogurt. These are sacred objects, offerings in an ancient and primitive ritual. In this poem we can clearly see that Snyder, too, is reborn: the birth of Kai energizes him by drawing something from deep inside him which he may not have known existed. As Snyder relates, Masa, Kai, and their friend Non, "In the green garden light," stay in the house, "making a new world of ourselves / around this life" (34). Surely, through Snyder's marriage to Masa and the birth of his son, he has most deeply regarded the "waves" of energy manifest in woman and found the "power within" himself.

    II   *"Looking at girls as mothers or daughters or sisters*
                     for a change of view."

Huck Finn did not realize that, when he rejected the offers of Aunt Sally and struck off for "the Territory," he was responding to an ancient urge to remain savage and not become domesticated. Rip Van Winkle, Junius Maltby in Steinbeck's *The Pastures of Heaven,* and all the other male outcasts of American literature have acted in similar fashion since they too have rejected the civilizing forces of the society of women. They shouldered their guns or fishing rods and headed for the hills. This theme is developed extensively by Ernest Hemingway in *Men Without Women* (1927) and adeptly criticized by Leslie Fiedler in *Love and Death in the American Novel* (1960). Although such literary works have been the basis for the sad parade of literature today concerning impotence, unhappy marriages, and infidelity in suburbia, they have not influenced the most recent poetry of Gary Snyder. To Snyder, women are no threat; they do not adopt or "sivilize" him; instead, they are seen, as mentioned above, the source of a power prior to civilization.

Throughout the body of his work, Snyder's interest in feminine psychology, in its influence on culture, and in the varying conceptions of the role of women in different societies is evident. In particular, such basic feminine functions as menstruation and childbirth which have been quite troubling to most men have greatly interested Snyder, as can be noted from the discussion above. For example, in "Praise for Sick Women" *(Riprap)*, Snyder tries, as he once said, "to put [himself] in a place where [he] could understand the archaic menstrual taboos in regard to the growth and conception of the fetus."[11] His empathy and his sense of identification with woman's biological and cultural position are clear in the lines, "All women are wounded / . . . you young girls / First caught with the gut cramp . . ." *(Riprap*, 5). After calling "kali / shakti" (the combined manifestation of Mahadevi, the most powerful Hindu goddess, representing life and death), Snyder asks, "Where's hell then?" And he answers, "In the moon. / In the change of the moon . . . ."

His sympathy and his understanding of the biological conditions which inevitably shape a woman's life are great. From his anthropological studies, he draws specific knowledge of menstrual taboo to illustrate the link between biological exigency and cultural subjection. Snyder in "Praise for Sick Women" implies how fear and awe of the procreative process influenced the development of ritual in the hope of controlling the experience. In Section 2, the poem relates the belief that apples sour when gazed upon by a menstruating woman; and then he describes other effects:

> Blossoms fail the bough,
> Soil turn bone-white: wet rice,
> Dry rice, die on the hillslope. (4)

As a consequence, the primitive admonition to "wounded" women to gather purifiers and to keep away from the area where food is prepared follows: "Gather punk wood and sour leaf / Keep out of our kitchen" (5). Snyder concludes the poem with a reference to the Amerindian practice of seclusion during menstruation: the woman was sent to a bark shack outside the camp where she "Crouched from sun, five days, / Blood dripping through crusted thighs."

More significant, however, than this relation of anthropological detail to the menstrual period is Snyder's depiction of the feminine state of consciousness during menstruation. His imagery in "Praise for Sick Women" is delicate, warm, and bright: "Sick women / Dreaming of long-legged dancing in light" (15). In these lines, the poet expresses the yearning of women for freedom. Snyder depicts their grace and beauty; gives infinite attention to detail in the lines, "Your garden plots, your bright fabrics, / Clever ways to carry children / Hide / a beauty like season or tide"; and he vividly portrays the creativity and resourcefulness of women who "gather berries, . . ./ Turn white roots from humus, crack nuts on stone. . . ." Even though women are politically dominated by men and although they are shaped by the biological realities of their own bodies, Snyder suggests that women are in control: they grow and cook the food, make the clothes, and have the children. In this extension of maternal care to the domestication of plants and animals, noted by the historian Gordon Childe, [12] is where real female power lies. As psychologist G. Devereaux in "The Psychology of Feminine Genital Bleeding" points out, the restrictions placed upon menstruating women "clearly indicate where genuine power rests: in women, who propagate the species. . . ."[13]

In "Praise for Sick Women," the poet's sensitivity to feminine sensibility in general is present; and his description of the woman's bodily movements during love-making is especially adept:

> head held sideways
> Arm out softly, touching,
> A difficult dance to do, but not in mind.
>
> Hand on sleeve: she holds leaf turning
>   in sunlight on spiderweb;
> Makes him flick like trout through shallows
> Builds into ducks and cold marshes
> Sucks out the quiet: bone rushes in

Behind the cool pupil a knot grows
Sudden roots sod him and solid him
Rain falls from skull-roof mouth is awash
    with small creeks
Hair grows, tongue tenses out — and she

Quick turn of the head: back glancing, one hand
Fingers smoothing the thigh, and he sees. (4)

The imagery of this passage captures the delicacy of movement and the modesty of women. Since emphasis is also placed on tactile imagery, the reader feels the touching, the movements, the dance that is love-making. Although Snyder's perception of women might be considered traditional, even conservative, it is, nonetheless, revealing and evocative. "The female is fertile, and discipline / (contra naturam) only / confuses her," writes Snyder. Thus, she is associated with flowing water, cold marshes, rain inside one's skull — in short, with the imagery of fertility and of the unconscious. Through his contact with woman, the poet "sees."

Snyder has written in his journal " — True insight a love-making hovering between the void and the immense worlds of creation. To symbolically represent *Prajna* [wisdom] as female is right" (*Earth House Hold*, 22). And he has stated in his thesis in regard to the quest myth that "Woman . . . symbolizes 'the totality of what can be known' . . ." (97). To Snyder, woman and the act of love-making become a field for experiencing the universe as a sacrament. The lover's bed, according to Snyder, is the place in which contemporary man enacts the dances and ritual dramas of the primitive. Like D. H. Lawrence, Snyder conceives women as being not only more responsive to the unconscious but closer to the source of life. Thus, discipline, an abstraction used here in the sense of force or rigidity, is contrary to the workings of nature and only confuses women. Expanding on this psychological difference between the sexes, Snyder's poem suggests that man is trapped in his intellect and does not listen to his body; as a result, he loses contact with the world he lives in. On the other hand, Snyder seemingly suggests that woman, although rooted in the earth, drifts like a cloud through life. This seeming paradox is resolved by the imagery of the poem, for both the imagery of the soil and the dance coalesce to produce this effect of lightness and floating. Women lead men to insight; they teach men to dance.

Snyder's interest in women, again similar to Lawrence's, also includes their relationship to economics and politics. Snyder's hope for social revolution centers on the woman's place in society. Very much interested in Lewis Henry Morgan's work on the matrilineal Iroquois (1851) and his book, *Ancient Society* (1877), which represented a broad theory of social evolution and consequently motivated Friedrich Engels to write in 1884 *Origins of the Family, Private Property and the State*, Snyder has noted "the revolutionary implications of the custom of matrilineal descent . . ." (*Earth House Hold*, 105). Clearly, Snyder regards matrilineal descent as innately more creative and as free: "Civilization so far has implied a patriarchal, patrilineal family. Any other system allows too much creative sexual energy to be released into channels which are 'unproductive'" (*Earth House Hold*, 106). Thus, Snyder concludes that sexual repression and the subjugation of women are linked and, in essence, political. In this regard, Section 1 of "Praise for Sick Women" dramatizes the primitive power of woman as mother, teacher, and seer. Section 2, which describes the fear and subjugation of this female power to man and to his adherence to logic, indicates the cultural and ultimately political suppression of instinct. This Snyder presents poetically by indicating the natural basis in female biology which facilitates this control.

"Praise for Sick Women," however, was not written as a polemic or as an apology; it is predominantly a work of art written in praise of womankind. And Snyder's attraction to and adoration of woman is evident in this poem in which he marvels over the beauty of her body and movements, her resourcefulness, and he displays her courage and ability to endure pain. Indeed, the reader learns that Snyder's love and respect are boundless. In this way and in certain others, Snyder's work is similar, as suggested above, to that of the poet and novelist D. H. Lawrence.

III   *"lopsided intuitions"*

Although Snyder was not influenced by Lawrence's literary style, Lawrence's ideas and general sensibility, especially as presented in the novels, excited the teenage Snyder; for Lawrence was a man who was profoundly knowledgable about matters which excited Snyder — women, sex, and Indians. In regard to this latter interest in Indians, Snyder has stated, "I start from someone like Lawrence."[14] While at Lincoln High School in Portland, Oregon, Snyder, as he relates in a recent letter, read the works of D. H. Lawrence.[15] And, while at sea on his first trip to Japan, musing about the tropical birds and fields of plankton, Snyder remembered reading Lawrence's *Aaron's Rod*. Certainly, Snyder considers with approval "Lawrence and his fantastic, accurate, lopsided intuitions" (*Earth House Hold*, 32).

Lawrence believed the white race was going mad or, in the words of Gary Snyder, that "the race is going somewhere else."[16] In Lawrence's *The Plumed Serpent*, a novel discussing the revival of the ancient Amerindian gods of Mexico, the novelist editorializes: "That which is aboriginal in America still belongs to the way of the world before the Flood . . . . In America . . . the mental-spiritual life of white people suddenly flourishes like a great weed let loose in virgin soil. Probably it will as quickly wither. . . . And after that, the living result will be a new germ, a new conception of human life, that will arise from the fusion of the old-blood-and vertebrate consciousness with the white man's present mental-spiritual consciousness."[17] This concern over the development of the race, the mixture of "bloods," and the health and diversity of the "gene pool" has interested Snyder for some time. References to this topic increasingly appear in his public readings and lectures. In "Clear-Cut" (*Manzanita*), a recent poem, he suggests, much as Lawrence did, that human diversity is the key to world health.

Although influenced by this idea of Lawrence, Snyder does not swallow Lawrence's position whole. In contrast to Snyder's religious relationship to archaic knowledge and the primitive, Lawrence's "new conception of human life" seems in essence cynical and manipulative. Whereas Snyder regards the archaic as offering knowledge and the aboriginal as a more primary form of insight — that is, Snyder sees himself in this regard as student — Lawrence reacts more like a contemporary consumer. Ancient ways are purchased and worn like costumes; primitives are placed strategically for effect; and a certain humorlessness exists in Lawrence's work. Nonetheless, Lawrence should not be judged too severely since his exploring this new territory of primitive potency and instinctual life made him one of the first writers after Jean-Jacques Rousseau to take the primitive seriously, and Snyder gives him credit for this contribution to thought.

In another respect, Lawrence may also have had another influence upon Snyder; for although Snyder probably read most of Lawrence's social novels, he only mentions *Aaron's Rod* in his journal. He writes about the novel as if it impressed him as a youth more than the others. To suggest, therefore, that Snyder probably identified with Aaron Sisson — as many readers have with Hemingway's Nick Adams, Farrell's Studs Lonigan, or even Twain's Huck Finn — is not farfetched. Aaron Sisson, the central character in the novel, like Snyder, has a working-class background, and he abandons his family to search for integrity and self-hood as Snyder relates he himself did in "Tasting the Snow" (*The Back Country*, 92). Although Sisson is in the final analysis a pathetic creature who is used by everyone and who is essentially a drifter with no set convictions, this picaresque hero must have evoked something deep inside the young Gary Snyder — dreams of travel, the hope of meeting exotic and rich people, new ideas and action — reminiscent of the stories of the tramps and bindle stiffs of Snyder's Depression youth and foreshadowing the concerns of the "Beats," who like Snyder, would go "on the road" in the 1950's.

While inspired by Lawrence's general revolutionary tendencies, Snyder must have been forced to admit the existence of obvious ambivalence and disenchantment in Lawrence's novels of social change. Cynical in outlook, Lawrence was unable to accept his own occasionally astute conclusions. For example, in *The Plumed Serpent* he displays his awareness that social revolution can lead to dictatorship, but he seems unable to know what to do with this insight. Unlike Snyder, who saw this danger in Lawrence's thought, Lawrence seems to have distrusted human nature. An elitist, as was Pound, Lawrence's solution as presented in *The Plumed Serpent* is to create a "higher, responsible, conscious class," one reminiscent of Lilly's position in *Aaron's Rod*. This class of priests would manipulate the symbols through which people lived, and such an elitist approach to government would inevitably lead to social control. Ironically, concerns such as mercy, liberation, and peace, so important to Snyder, are absent from Lawrence's stark behavioristic approach to community.

Lawrence certainly does not portray Snyder's peaceful revolution of consciousness discussed in "Buddhism and the Coming Revolution" in *Earth House Hold*. In fact, Snyder's discussion in this essay concerning the distortion of human potential by the deliberate fostering of craving seems quite relevant in this instance, almost written in response to Lawrence. Clearly, Snyder does not succumb to the extremism of men such as Skinner and Lawrence. Aware that turmoil is an inevitable aspect of social upheaval, Snyder is more hopeful and less afraid. In addition, Snyder's Buddhism, with its central belief in emptiness, precludes pessimism, or even for that matter optimism, in the contemporary sense. As Snyder writes in his revolutionary broadside "Four Changes" now collected in *Turtle Island*, "knowing that nothing need be done, is where we begin to move from." Snyder was aware as a young man that, although serious and genuinely concerned with affecting change, Lawrence was not a full-blown revolutionary. While intellectually supporting change, Lawrence seems to have been emotionally unable to deal with social flux and its consequences. Always remaining somehow detached from the people and the causes he forwarded, his alienation, typical of postwar writers, and so different from Snyder's sense of connection with all life forms, continued until his death. Both physically and psychically Lawrence remained an exile.

In another area of interest, however, Snyder and Lawrence are closer. Lawrence, like Snyder, was fascinated with women and sexuality. In his work, Lawrence delved into the nature of love and the respective shapes of the male and female psyche. Although a bit melodramatic and chaste by contemporary standards, Lawrence in his stories and novels created a flow of genuine erotic passion that had been damned for the average reader since the Victorian era. Less stylized and more openly erotic, yet taking its example from Lawrence's literature, Snyder's love poetry captures all the aspects of love-making — the tastes, smells, gestures, and touches — so sweet to Lawrence. Copious examples of Snyder's early love poetry are to be found in *The Back Country:* "Night," "Nanao Knows," "Lying in Bed on a Late Morning," "The Truth Like the Belly of a Woman Turning," "How Many Times," and others. In his love poetry, Snyder writes as did Lawrence of self-abandonment and total involvement.

Snyder's amazing understanding of a woman's psychology and needs, as well as those of her male lover, is exhibited in numerous poems such as "Song of the Tangle," "Song of the Slip," and "Song of the View," which are in *Regarding Wave* and which were originally published in "Eight Songs of Clouds and Water." In these poems, Snyder's matter-of-fact, anti-Romantic approach to the

human body and to sexuality is evident. More open and less com-
pulsive than Lawrence, Snyder writes in "Song of the Slip":

> SLEPT
> folded in girls
> feeling their folds; whorls;
> the lips, leafs,
> of the curling   soft-sliding
> serpent-sleep dream. (*Regarding Wave*, 15)

This description is lusty and joyous. Snyder takes great delight in
the physical properties of his female accomplices, "roaring and far-
ing" (15), he simply "moves in and makes home in the whole," the
vagina that he enters. Although this poem may shock some readers,
Snyder's respect and reverence for womankind and for the female
genitalia are undeniable.

Another love poem, "Song of the View," also lacks sexual compli-
cation. Presenting erotic art somewhat similar to the poems of
Catullus, or to those of his Jacobean imitator Ben Jonson, the poem,
although quite explicit, is neither obscene nor pornographic. Here,
there is none of the teasing quality of seventeenth-century Cavalier
verse, or the longing intellectuality of John Donne. Snyder writes:

> O! cunt
>
> that which you suck in —
>   to yourself, that you
>   hold
>   there,
>   hover over,
>   excellent emptiness your
>   whole flesh is wrappt around,
>   the
> hollow you bear
>   to
>   bear,
>
> shows its power and place
>
> in the grace of your glance (*Regarding Wave*, 16)

Snyder's perception of the vagina's mothering capacities for the
male organ develops the sense of peace, warmth, security, and

completion that he associates with love. Although Snyder was at one time responsive to the works of Theodor Reik which stress the importance of orgasm, he is not writing just about sexual climax; for, as he states in "Song of the Taste," love is "Kissing the lover in the mouth of bread: / lip to lip." Love is, therefore, an act of communion like "Eating each other's seed . . ." (*Regarding Wave*, 17). Sounding somewhat like the poet e. e. cummings, Snyder quotes an unknown source in his journal: " 'Love is a process of the incomprehensible human soul . . . but still only a process. The process should work to a completion. . . . The completion of the process of love is the arrival at a state of simple, pure self-possession, for man and woman. Only that' " (*Earth House Hold*, 32).

Knowledgable in Tantric Buddhism and sexual yoga, Snyder was also to write in "Dharma Queries" of the ritualist aspects of love, or of love as an act of worship: "To follow the ancient path in company with a lover means both must have practiced the lonely yogas and wanderings, and then seek the center of the individual-body and group-body mandala; dedicating their two bodies to the whole network; the man evoking the Goddess in the girl on suitable occasions and worshiping her" (*Earth House Hold*, 133).

In this respect, the early description of sexual love as worship seen in "The Plum Blossom Poem" and in "Beneath My Hand and Eye the Distant Hills, Your Body" (*The Back Country*, pp. 108–09) is completed in "Song of the Tangle" (*Regarding Wave*, 14). This more recent poem, describing *yab-yum* (form of Tibetan sitting coitus) in a Japanese temple, is more concise stylistically and less complicated intellectually. In "Beneath My Hand . . . " Snyder writes, "Where 'I' / follow by hand and eye / the swimming limit of your body. / As when vision idly dallies on the hills / Loving what it feeds on" (109). In "Song of the Tangle," the same connection is made between body and land, between love and the cycle of nature. However, it is made more adeptly. The details are fewer and more simple; more is left out; the effect is more profound and satisfying:

> Two thigh hills hold us at the fork
> round mount center
>
> . . .
>
> calm tree halls
> the sun past the summit

> heat sunk through the vines,
> twisted sasa

> cicada singing,
> swirling in the tangle

> the tangle of the thigh

> the brush
> through which we push (14)

Clearly an early influence on the thought and expression of Gary Snyder, the work of D. H. Lawrence offered the example of a more appreciative approach to the primitive and to the workings of the unconscious; and especially trail-breaking was his response to feminine psychology. Through his frank, if at times stilted depiction of sexuality, Lawrence was to have an initial, if not lasting influence on many young poets and writers such as Gary Snyder. If Lawrence's social ideas seem adolescent and untenable in this time, we must still give him credit where it is due. If not a great poet or social thinker, Lawrence was an important liberator, pointing out the path of greater freedom of expression for younger poets and writers to follow.

CHAPTER 8

Drawing the Line

IN December, 1968, Gary Snyder returned to the United States with his Japanese wife Masa and son Kai. After living briefly in a small apartment on Pine Street in San Francisco, where his second son Gen was born, he moved with his family to land he had bought in the foothills of the Sierras. In an interview conducted by Bruce Cook in 1971, just prior to the move, Snyder relates: "It's just some acres of wilderness I bought with a cabin on it. But I want to get us out there, so we can begin to learn to break the habits of dependence. It's important to me. I think it will mean more consciousness, more awareness."[1] With the accomplishment of nearly twenty years' work behind him, Snyder in his early forties, began another phase of his career.

The perambulations of *The Back Country* ended, and the role of father and husband and the experience of domestic life developed and elevated to the heights of art in *Regarding Wave,* Snyder's concern for roots and search for sources deepened. His next and most recent work is *Turtle Island,* whose title, so Snyder writes in the Introductory Note, is "the old / new name for the continent, based on many creation myths of the people who have been living here for millenia, and reapplied by some of them to 'North America' in recent years . . . an idea found world-wide, of the earth, or cosmos even, sustained by a great turtle or serpent-of-eternity." He adds, it is "A name: that we may see ourselves more accurately on this continent. . . ." He concludes, "Hark again to those roots, to see our ancient solidarity, and then to the work of being together on Turtle Island." Or, as Snyder presents this idea poetically in "What Happened Here Before,"

> Turtle Island swims
> in the ocean-sky swirl-void

> biting its tail while worlds go
> on-and-off
> winking. (*Turtle Island*, 80)

Turtle Island is composed of four sections: "Manzanita," the lead section, was first published in limited edition in 1972; "Magpie's Song" and "For the Children" contain many new poems; and "Plain Talk" is a collection of recent essays and miscellaneous prose pieces about ecological subjects. Although *Turtle Island* continues to explore the theme of familial love and harmony ("The Bath," "The Egg," "Bedrock"), it also contains not only little rhyming poems probably written by Snyder for his sons ("The Uses of Light," "The Wild Mushroom") but also poems that exhibit Snyder's mystical relation to the land ("For Nothing," "By Frazier Creek Falls," "Rain in Alleghany," "On San Gabriel Ridges"). However, a substantial amount of *Turtle Island* comes from a different level of Snyder's creative mind than these other types of subjects. In this respect, this different group is similar to the short work, *The Fudo Trilogy* (1973) which contains only three poems: "Spel Against Demons," first published in *Manzanita* (1972) and later collected in *Turtle Island;* "Smokey the Bear Sutra," a work already mentioned, and first published as a broadside; and "The California Water Plan," discussed in Chapter 5 as a recently added section of *Mountains and Rivers Without End.*

Basically, the poems in *Turtle Island* (and in *The Fudo Trilogy*) seem written more to teach than to edify. Some are as unusually abstract as "Song to the Raw Material" *(Manzanita)*, which, though omitted from *Turtle Island*, explores the nature of "meta-ecology or meta-economics." In short, *Turtle Island* is a didactic and even at times a dogmatic book that contains prose and poetry that are the result of deeply held views. In this respect, *Turtle Island* continues the revolutionary themes of *Myths & Texts* and *Earth House Hold;* and the poems themselves exceed in length and impact those in the two sections ("Long Hair" and "Target Practice") that were added to the 1970 edition of *Regarding Wave.* Taken with his new role of the poet as public figure, Snyder presents in *Turtle Island* the work of a deeply socially concerned poet, one whose opinions and perceptions, now matured and tested, are grounded in close observation and in knowledge of how things work. Indeed, Snyder presents his own development as a poet in "Toward Climax": "maturity. stop and think. draw on the mind's / stored richness. memory, dream, half-digested / image of your life" *(Turtle Island,* 84). Or, as he states in "Night Herons" in referring to his own veteran status and his return to San Francisco, the scene of his earlier activism,

> How could the
> night herons ever come back?
> to this noisy place on the bay.
> like me.
> the joy of all the beings
> is in being
> older and tougher and eaten
> up. *(Turtle Island,* 36)

I   *"(relatively) permanent things"*

In its social radicalism, in its cyclic evocation, and in its occasional accusatory tone, *Turtle Island* resembles the shorter poems of another California poet, Robinson Jeffers. Jeffer's "Inhumanism," similar to Snyder's ecological vision, is evident in "The Purse-Seine":

> We have geared the machines and locked all together
> into interdependence; we have built the great cities; now
> There is no escape. We have gathered vast populations incapable
> of free survival, insulated
> From the strong earth, each person in himself helpless, on all
> dependent. The circle is closed, and the net
> Is being hauled in.[2]

Both Snyder and Jeffers, like other Western American writers, look with disapproval on "progress" and on the general drift of Western civilization; that is, its unconscious desire to render the wild world tame and to bend nature to its will. The poets see man as full of pride and his institutions as insignificant in the vastness of the universe. In "Milton by Firelight", Snyder states,

> In ten thousand years the Sierras
> Will be dry and dead, home of the scorpion.
> Ice-scratched slabs and bent trees.

> No paradise, no fall,
> Only the weathering land
> The wheeling sky. . . . (*Riprap*, 7–8)

In "Tor House," Jeffers, describing the house on the wild California coast which he had fashioned with his own hands from "sea-worn granite," writes:

> If you should look for this place after a handful of lifetimes:
> Perhaps of my planted forest a few
> May stand yet . . .
> But if you should look in your idleness after ten thousand years;
> It is the granite knoll on the granite
> And lava tongue in the midst of the bay. . . . [3]

In these two poems, both poets display their "cosmic consciousness," for man and his achievements are placed in perspective. Human life is impermanent and, in the sense presented in these two poems, relatively insignificant. These conservative, preservationist attitudes of Jeffers are presented in "The Coast-Road":

>   I too
> Believe that the life of men who ride horses, herders of cattle on
>   the mountain pastures, plowers of remote
> Rock-narrowed farms in poverty and freedom, is a good life. At
>   the far end of those loops of road
> Is what will come and destroy it, a rich and vulgar and bewildered
>   civilization dying at the core. . . . [4]

Snyder who admits the significant influence "not in style, but in tone,"[5] of Jeffers on his work, states that all thru that period [early 1950's] I was also reading Robinson Jeffers";[6] and he writes in a similar tone in his more recent poem, "Civilization,"

> Those are the people who do complicated things.
>
>   they'll grab us by the thousands
>   and put us to work.
> World's going to hell, with all these
>   villages and trails.
> Wild duck flocks aren't
>   what they used to be. (*Regarding Wave*, 84)

In "The Trade' " Snyder describes "throngs of people" in discount stores "trading all their precious time / for things" (*Regarding Wave*, 47). More recently he develops this theme of decadent civilization and its destructive consequences in *Turtle Island*. In "Facts," Snyder relates quite bluntly that "The U.S. has 6% of the world's population; consumes ⅓ the energy annually consumed in the world" (*Turtle Island*, 31). In "The Dead by the Side of the Road," with a fierceness similar to that of Jeffers in "Hurt Hawks," Snyder asks, "How did a great Red-tailed Hawk / come to lie — all stiff and dry — / on the shoulder of / Interstate 5?" (*Turtle Island*, 7). In another poem, these spiritual interests take on political form when, in "The Call of the Wild," Snyder portrays the contemporary sensibility which prompts a "heavy old man" to "call the Government trapper" because a coyote's singing disturbs him; the hippies, fresh from the cities, to sell their virgin cedar trees, "the tallest trees in miles," because a logger told them "Trees are full of bugs"; and the Air Force to continue to bomb the Viet Cong doggedly because "Defeat / is Un-American." To Snyder, such actions are "A war against earth"; and he adds, eerily reminiscent of Jeffers' "The Purse-Seine," that "I would like to say / Coyote is forever / Inside you. But it's not true" (*Turtle Island*, 23).

Snyder's shocking realization of America's profligacy is also evident in other poems in *Turtle Island*. "Black Mesa Mine #1" is a poem concerned with the strip mining of sacred Navajo lands ("ancient mother mountain," [67]). "LMFBR" describes the threat to life of the liquid metal, fast-breeder reactor and of the indestructible trash such as aluminum cans and PVC pipe which "don't exactly burn, don't quite rot, / flood over us" (67). In "Affluence," aptly titled, the poet relates how he found in the woods "two sixteen foot good butt logs . . . ," left wastefully by loggers twenty years before. Citizens are now, concludes Snyder, "paying the price somebody didn't pay" (50).

More directly and with greater optimism, Snyder relates in "Tomorrow's Song" how the United States, because of its mindless rapacity, "lost its mandate" and "Turtle Island returned" (77). He looks with pleasure, much as Jeffers did, to this future era when people will "need no fossil fuel" and will "grow strong on less" (77). As he relates in "The Jemez Pueblo Ring," modern civilizations crumble ("In forty years the apartments useless and torn down" [76]), but the "ancient solidarity" and ways, which Snyder mentions in the Introductory Note to *Turtle Island*, remain. Or, as he states with finality in "It Pleases" when he is describing the flight of a large bird soaring above the capitol in Washington, D.C., "And the center, / The center of power is nothing! / Nothing here." "The world does what it pleases" (44).

In the Foreword to *The Selected Poetry of Robinson Jeffers*, Jeffers writes, ". . . poetry must deal with things that a reader two thousand years away could understand and be moved by." Jeffers continues, "Poetry must concern itself with (relatively) permanent things."[7] In the biographical section appended to the anthology, *A Controversy of Poets*, the editors, Paris Leary and Robert Kelly, include a statement made by Snyder for the Paterson Society in 1961. Snyder, sounding very much like Jeffers, writes, "America five hundred years ago was clouds and birds, miles of bison, endless forests and grass and clear water. Today it is the tired ground of the world's dominant culture."[8] Snyder's activism, of course, goes farther than that of Jeffers whose personality and inclinations were different. Snyder's "I Went Into the Maverick Bar," "Front Lines," and "The Real Work," could not have been written by Jeffers because of their insistence on action. Nonetheless, Jeffers' influence on the works of Gary Snyder, especially in regard to subject matter and tone, is worth mentioning; but more intensive explorations should prove fruitful in future studies of the works of Gary Snyder.

II   *"What is to be done"*

The poems in *Turtle Island* clearly represent the mind of Gary Snyder in the 1970's, and *Turtle Island* indicates more about the drift of Snyder's philosophic development than about the "increased suppleness of style, . . . loosened rhythms and diction" that reviewer John R. Carpenter perceived in *Regarding Wave*.[9] Moreover, in *Turtle Island* Snyder has disproved reviewer Alan Brownjohn's earlier criticism that Snyder had ". . . retreated almost altogether to a neutrally observing position . . . ";[10] for *Turtle Island* is evidence of Snyder's flowering social conscience and of his continuation of a ministry of love and concern for one's fellow creatures and for the biosphere. In one sense, *Turtle Island* is the work of a veteran teacher; Snyder, acting in the role of *roshi*, offers his help, his instructions, his magic. In "For the Children," Snyder offers the advice, *"stay together / learn the flowers / go light"* (86). And, in "Ethnobotany," he suggests, "Taste all, and hand the knowledge down" (51). Surely, this most recent book is the presentation of what is essential for all mankind; for the reader is told in the "Source"

> To be in
> to the land
> . . .
>
> Up here
> out back
> drink deep
> that black light. (*Turtle Island*, 26)

Turtle Island is also a book of directions and instructions in poetic form. In *Turtle Island*, one finds spells and charms to protect against and to exorcize the demons which inhabit the American psyche, such as in "Spel Against Demons" (also collected in *The Fudo Trilogy*) and "Charms." One also finds references to archaic sources of strength and knowledge in "Anasazi" (Indians) and in "The Way West Underground" (ancient bear mythology). Prayers and poems are written in praise of life in "Prayer for the Great Family," "The Bath," and "Coyote Valley Spring"; and the cautionings of the gentle and concerned teacher appear in poems such as "The Great Mother," where not all who pass the "Great Mother's" chair receive only a stare: "Some she looks at their hands / To see what sort of savages they were" (*Turtle Island*, 20).

Whether Snyder is an earth, air, fire, water, space, or mind poet, as he outlines these types in "As For Poets," one cannot determine. Nonetheless, Snyder has found meaning in his own life; he offers it to the reader. In short, *Turtle Island* presents Snyder as poet-teacher and as a social activist who is talking calmly at one time, instructing at another, working for change in "Control Burn," showing "What is to be done" (9) in "I Went Into the Maverick Bar," or giving the battle cry against our society's destructiveness and materialism. In this anxious twentieth century, *Turtle Island* is a source of hope, peace, and benediction. Placed in the body of Snyder's work, *Turtle Island* evidences a heightened philosophical and political awareness. Indeed, Snyder seems to have found work to be accomplished, acceptance of his calling, and the willingness to

utilize his poetic talents in the cause of his strongly held convictions.
As he writes in "Front Lines," "Every pulse of the rot at the
heart / In the sick fat veins of Amerika / Pushes the edge up
closer —" (*Turtle Island*, 18). And Snyder concludes,

> Behind is a forest that goes to the Arctic
> And a desert that still belongs to the Piute
> And here we must draw
> Our line. (18)

CHAPTER 9

Conclusion

I   *Creating a New Culture*

SINCE the publication of Jack Kerouac's *The Dharma Bums* (1958)
and Alan Watt's *Beat Zen Square Zen and Zen* (1959), so much
has been written extolling the personality and life-style of Gary
Snyder that he is recognizably a man who commands respect. As
Charles Reznikoff states in 1970, Snyder "doesn't fake anything. He
has been there, and he takes us with him."[1] Nonetheless, since the
publication of *Earth House Hold* (1969), this tendency toward subjective, biographical response has accelerated. Such a turn of affairs
has given rise to an over-emphasis of the public figure Gary
Snyder — of Snyder as a culture-hero. A reviewer for *Time*, A. T.
Baker, in 1971 links Snyder with what he calls "THE CULT
POETS . . . more cherished for their life-styles than their verse."[2]
In *Glamour*, a national fashion magazine, Snyder is presented as one
of a number of "gurus" in 1970 who are "piping the tune" of eco-
activism.[3] Snyder's books have even been advertised in *The Whole
Earth Catalog* and are reviewed (1971) glowingly in the "hip,"
popular culture newspaper, *Rolling Stone*, whose reviewer relates
that "Snyder's been there."[4] This media picture of Snyder which
emerges is an unfortunate caricature that deemphasizes Snyder's
major role as an important poet.

It must be admitted, however, that, as Thomas Lyon indicates,
Snyder's participation in public events, such as the symposium
called "Changes" conducted in the late 1960's by *The City of San
Francisco Oracle* in which he participated with Alan Watts, Timothy
Leary, and Allen Ginsberg, indicates Snyder's uncontested position
as a leading figure of the subculture.[5] Snyder has used this prominence, however, as a platform for concerns which have less to do
with poetry than propaganda — a fact that may indicate that

Snyder's goals are diverse and complex; that he sees the art of poetry, as Thomas Parkinson has sensed, as "only one of a set of instruments in a spiritual quest. . . . "[6] It may also be true, therefore, that Snyder's work acts, as Parkinson states, "as a spiritual rather than technical force" for the young.[7] Indeed, the wholeheartedly enthusiastic response of youths to *Earth House Hold* indicate not only the validity of such an assertion but also that "Technical Notes & Queries to Fellow Dharma Revolutionaries" amounts to another guide book for a generation that hungers for "real" teachers and for practical knowledge about how to beat the system and to be freed from competition and needless acquisition. The power of this work which embodies the spiritual and social motives of those under thirty is apparent because Snyder is regarded by the searching and troubled young, who read little but listen and observe a great deal, as a religious teacher and model.

Another factor that creates Snyder's influence is the fact that the conception of poetry and the role of the poet has changed since the 1950's, especially in the minds of the young. The new concern is to relate to poetry more personally and to get something specifically from it. This refreshing pragmatism, if one wishes to see it as such, stresses in poetry its opportunities for learning and for self-awareness. In this respect, Snyder's life and poetry offer the reader a glowing example; for, like a good teacher, Snyder in *Earth House Hold* does not "harp" or "get windy." Timothy Baland observes in 1970, *Earth House Hold* "moves along like a stone skipping water, touching lightly . . . then sinking deep."[8] As a colleague, who is in his mid-twenties and who speaks for the undergraduate disillusioned by political scandal and war, states, "*Earth House Hold* is a source-book. It helps us to get back in touch. Snyder uses language to find out what it is to be human."[9]

Although it is understandable that some critics may observe with disapproval this unabashed "use" of poetry and the function of the poet to attain social ends, such superficial responses as those of Aleksandar Nejgebauer, who views Snyder in 1969 as a zealot living in a "dreamworld come true," would not seem to be grounded in a thorough reading of the poetry of Gary Snyder.[10] In such cases, one has the distinct impression that criticism has been based only on personal interview or, at best, on the reading of sections of *Earth House Hold* and possibly a few poems. Such facile and often irresponsible comment, however, is to be expected, when a poet becomes, for others, a media figure.

Beneath the bustle and turmoil of public discussion, the value of Snyder as poet remains. Of the quality and profundity of his work more thorough readers have been aware. One of the most astute and consistent critics of Snyder's work, Thomas Parkinson, while admittedly promoting the development of the image of Snyder as a "Renaissance Man," cautions casual readers that Snyder "presents a different set of references and beings," that his poetry creates a "different set of human possibilities." Unintentionally but effectively commenting about the problem of the over-emphasis of biographical data in interpreting the work of Gary Snyder, Parkinson writes in 1968, "He has effectively done something that for an individual is extremely difficult: he has created a new culture."[11] Although the impact of Snyder's personality and life-style at present lies heavily on much of the discussion of the poet and his work, his reputation, similar to that of other "literary personalities" reviled or over-praised in their lifetimes, will rest on his poetry; and his original contribution to the literature of this country will become evident.

II *Critical Overview*

Receiving the first flush of serious criticism in the 1960's, and scoring high on an informal poll of poets conducted by Kenneth Rexroth, Snyder's poetic reputation among his peers is well established; and such poets as James Dickey and Robert Bly have written insightful and sympathetic essays about his poetry. In discussing in 1961 the work of other notable poets, Dickey states that Snyder is "the best of them"; and he is "by far the most interesting of these poets that I have read."[12] In the following year, 1962, poet, critic, and translator Robert Bly reviewed the work of Snyder and in a thorough and extremely sympathetic essay attests to Snyder's originality. Bly identifies Snyder's celebration of physical life, his "superior sensitivity," his "humorous awareness," and his ability to laugh at himself.[13] Bly, who asserts that Snyder is "devout in the most elemental sense,"[14] states that he can no longer be lumped with the "Beat Poets" because his work "reveals the grave mind of a man who is highly civilized. . . ."[15] To another contemporary poet, Louis Simpson, writing in 1967, Snyder is one of the "true poets."[16]

A continuing stream of competent and often astute criticism of Snyder's poetry has been published. In reviewing Snyder's first book *Riprap* (1959), Robert Sward notes in 1960 Snyder's simplicity, honesty, and appeal to the senses. He calls the book "impressive," but he also offers some reservations in his praise. A few of the poems, he states, seem "a bit phony" with a sameness of tone, shape, and emotional range.[17] Thomas Parkinson reviews in 1960–61 Snyder's second book of poems, *Myths & Texts* (1960) and mentions that there is a "terrible sanity" about the work of Gary Snyder.[18] Anthropologist Dell Hymes points out in 1961 that *Myths & Texts* will play a significant cultural role for the future historian of folklore.[19] And Lisel Mueller in 1968 calls Snyder's collected poems, *A Range of Poems* (1966), "A remarkably solid book, strong and sharp. . . ."[20] In addition to David Kherdian's *A Biographical Sketch and Descriptive Checklist of Gary Snyder* (1965), later included in *Six San Francisco Poets*, the 1960's saw the publication of three substantial articles written by competent critics about the body of Snyder's poetry at that time. Richard Howard, who wrote " 'To Hold Both History and Wilderness in Mind': The Poetry of Gary Snyder," restated in 1965 much of what past reviewers Dickey and Bly had already written but he also offered some valuable insights in his own right, notably Snyder's organicism.[21] In the fall of 1968, Thomas Lyon published "Gary Snyder, a Western Poet" in which he discussed in greater detail the idea first stated by Robert Bly that Snyder's poetry exhibits the workings of the "Western literary imagination" with its roots in the mythic consciousness of the American Indian.[22] And in "The Poetry of Gary Snyder," published in 1968, Thomas Parkinson developed points he had first sketched in "After the Beat Generation." Although aware of the "unanimity" of Snyder's poems, Parkinson believes that such a complaint could have been registered against Blake, Whitman, and Lawrence; Snyder "has a gift for quiet, untroubled, accurate observation with occasional leaps to genuine eloquence."[23] In a subsequent review of *Earth House Hold* and *Regarding Wave*, published in 1971–72, Parkinson adds that, when Snyder "is in the grip of a major principle. . . . He becomes the agent of a voice, that of common experience. . . . The superficial aspects are easy to imitate or ridicule, but what is fundamental has a life well beyond the particular."[24]

So far in the 1970's, Snyder's work has usually been received with favor. Thomas Parkinson has reviewed *Earth House Hold* and *Regarding Wave* as mentioned above, and John Carpenter, writing for *Poetry* in 1972 has called *Regarding Wave* "excellent"[25] and has noted its increased suppleness of style. Roy E. Teele in 1971 has discussed the influence of the Japanese poetic journal on sections of *Earth House Hold*;[26] and Daniel Jaffe, writing in the *Saturday Review* in 1971 has stated that *Regarding Wave* is a "book of connections."[27] More importantly, four significant articles have been written which were published in 1970 and which were obviously written under the influence of the so-called "Ecology Movement." These articles discuss Snyder as a nature poet and as an eco-activist. In "A Secular Pilgrimage," which discusses the work of three contemporary poets, Wendel Berry states that Snyder is the most austere poet and the one most willing to venture farthest from the human assumptions and enclosures.[28] Charles Altieri discusses in "Gary Snyder's Lyric Poetry: Dialectic as Ecology" Snyder's "ecological intention," which makes us "appreciate the balance in our lives."[29] Thomas Lyon also traces "The Ecological Vision of Gary Snyder."[30] In another article, Sherman Paul discusses Snyder's evolving radicalism, from passivism and withdrawal in the 1950's to activism and communitarianism in the 1960's and 1970's.[31] And most recently, both published in 1975, the *Mountain Gazette* and *The New Republic* have printed laudatory articles on Snyder and his work in response to his earning the Pulitzer Prize for Poetry (1975).[32]

III   *Comment*

Snyder has recently mentioned that the direction of his future work after the completion of *Mountains and Rivers Without End* will be religious and philosophical. He has also stated that after that work has been completed, he may donate his books to the local library and retire to the anonymity of friends and family life in the mountains. This desire and such a life are, of course, in the true Oriental style. However, if Snyder ends his poetic career after this decade, it would even then be premature to make any final pronouncements. Although the figure of Gary Snyder as a man may still overshadow that of Snyder the poet, cetain *tentative* statements can now be made. First of all, Snyder's reputation as a poet rests at present on *Myths & Texts*, his most complete work; on a few excellent poems from *Riprap*, *The Back Country*, and *Turtle Island;* on the cycle of poems in *Regarding Wave* first published in limited edition in 1969 by The Windhover Press; and especially on the more recent sections where Snyder's work reaches synthesis in his *magnum opus*, *Mountains and Rivers Without End*. In these poems, one finds directiness and simplicity of statement, clarity and brillance of mind, and profundity and depth of emotional range. In these instances, Snyder's is a poetry of incredible power and beauty.

The reader is particularly moved by "Mid-August At Sourdough Mountain Lookout," "The Late Snow & Lumber Strike of the Summer of Fifty-four," "Praise for Sick Women," "A Stone Garden," and "Riprap." These poems from *Riprap* (1959) are some of Snyder's earliest work, and they have been discussed at length in this study. Also significant are Snyder's trail-crew poems, also published in *Riprap*. "Piute Creek," in which "All the junk that goes with being human / Drops away" *(Riprap*, 6), and "Above Pate Valley," in which Snyder describes how he camped "On a hill snowed all but summer" (9) present a new kind of poetry with a different and truly American setting, the high country of the American West. In *Riprap* Snyder has created a poem as fresh and clear as the mountain stream he describes in "Water," in which he immersed his head, "Eyes open aching from the cold and faced a trout" (10).

Myths & Texts (1960), many readers' favorite work, is, as yet, Snyder's most complete and most unified book. This is not a collection of poems organized around a catchy title, as to a certain extent are *Riprap* and *The Back Country*, no matter how perfect some of their individual poems. *Myths & Texts* coheres perfectly. As discussed earlier in this study, all three of its sections relate specifically to one another, and there is a definite progression and feeling of completion while reading this book. Like "The Waste Land," which influenced its composition, *Myths & Texts* makes an over-all comment on our society and will probably stand the test of time. Within this work are individual poems of startling beauty and insight, for example, "Poem 2" from "Logging," in which Snyder relates his own complicity in the destruction of the forests. He states that "San

Francisco 2×4s / were the woods around Seattle" (4). Snyder was born and lived in San Francisco and such an insight is painful for him to share. The "Hunting" poems such as "this poem is for deer," are particularly moving in their beautiful and sensitive portrayal of the nonhuman beings which inhabit this planet: "Picasso's fawn, Issa's fawn, / Deer on the autumn mountain / Howling like a wise man . . . Keeping the human soul from care" (25).

Of particular note in *The Back Country* (1968) is "A Berry Feast," written to commemorate a summer spent with good friends in the woods of the Pacific Northwest. It is a saucy poem, filled with zest for life, written by Snyder while in a trickster-like mood. Also significant are the many simple songs of peace and happiness, such as "Marin-an" in which the poet listens to the people of middle America driving their cars to work. The "Kali" poems are also notable, as mentioned earlier in this study for their frank exploration of the demonic potential in man and in the poet in particular. And the poems in "Far East," inspired by Snyder's travels and studies in Japan are particularly important as well as poignant. "Six Years" adeptly portrays the rhythm of the poet's Zen studies. And "Yase: September" succinctly captures the essence of old Japan, embodied in the character of "Old Mrs. Kawabata," who "out of a mountain / of grass and thistle" saved a few dusty stalks of blue flower and kindly put them in Snyder's kitchen "in a jar" (37). In a similar manner, "The Public Bath" through a quick succession of images recreates a world so mysterious and fascinating to Westerners.

Turtle Island (1974), Snyder's most recent book, and *Regarding Wave* (1970) collect many poems which extend and complete themes and subjects treated in earlier works. For example, both books are concerned with social revolution and the search for alternate sources of energy. The cycle of poems from *Regarding Wave* concerning the birth of Snyder's first son, Kai, completes the poem "Praise for Sick Women" from *Riprap*. These four beautiful poems, describing the growth of Kai from conception until after birth move further into the mystical experience that is birth and life: "Kai. / born again" (33). "Song of the Taste" from *Regarding Wave*, possibly Snyder's most perfect poem, finishes his development of the idea of eating, first described in the "Hunting" section of *Myths & Texts* and later in the many "food" poems in *The Back Country*: "A Berry Feast" and "Oysters," for example. It seems that in "Song of the Taste," in which the reader learns how he draws "on life of living" (17), Snyder has reached the farthest extension and expression possible of this experience. The effect of this poem on the reader is startling. *Turtle Island*, with its lead section "Manzanita," which was first published separately in 1972, also develops old as well as new material. "The Bath" presents a warm and sensuous description of Snyder's family, joyously bathing in the sauna: "we / wash each other, / *this is our body*" (13). Always a favorite of audiences at Snyder's public readings, this poem is a more human and mature statement of the subject and sentiment of "The Public Bath," cited above, published in *The Back Country*. Other poems exploring the nature of energy often reach the height of mystical expression. "Without," "Source," "For Nothing," and especially "By Frazier Creek Falls" capture an awareness in language usually denied to less sensitive and articulate men. In "By Frazier Creek Falls" Snyder writes, "This living flowing land / is all there is, forever / We *are* it / it sings through us — " (41).

And finally, in *Mountains and Rivers Without End*, Snyder's continuing work, published periodically in sections, the reader can also see the gradual creation of a book, a collection of long poems, which may last for the same reasons that Whitman's *Leaves of Grass* lasts. Of particular note in this growing work are the sections titled "Bubbs Creek Haircut," "The Market," "The Blue Sky," and "The Hump-Backed Flute Player." The earlier poems, "Bubbs Creek Haircut" and "The Market," are clever and technically interesting: the poet takes liberties with the time sequence and describes exotic locales with a rapid and effective series of images. But it is in the last two sections mentioned in which this long work begins to achieve its potential. In "The Blue Sky" and "The Hump-Backed Flute Player" both Snyder's philosophic vision and incredibly adept technique coalesce. In these poems, Snyder has reached the pinnacle of his art, acting as poet-shaman, using language in its fullest magical properties — the poem as chant or mantra. Here, especially in "The Blue Sky," the poems not only describe healing, they actually heal. This is truly astonishing writing in which Snyder's poetry nearly transcends art. As Snyder writes:

> The Blue Sky
> The Blue Sky
>
> The Blue Sky
> is the land of

OLD MAN MEDICINE BUDDHA
where the Eagle
that Flies out of Sight

flies. (Mountains and Rivers Without End, 43–44)

Writing, in the main, within the Imagist tradition of Pound, Williams, and the Orient, Snyder's poetry is not solely Imagistic. The gradual development of his work from the crafted to the visionary poem, his interest in primitive oral poetry, and his recent allusions to Whitman, Duncan, and other mystical poets attest to this. Significantly influenced early in his career by the demands of Oriental nature poetry for precision, sharpness, and spontaneity, Snyder's movement into Imagism and later toward the "visionary" was assured when he began his study of Buddhism in college. Its influence on the mind of Gary Snyder is profound, and it is deepening as he matures. From the sometimes "easy" references of *Riprap* to the basis of his later more mature work, *Regarding Wave* and the later sections of *Mountains and Rivers Without End*, one finds this deepening of thought. However, since Buddhist theory is integral to these latter works, their richness and depth may be lost to those who do not have some knowledge of Buddhism. No poet in American literature has made Buddhist psychology so completely his own. Applied to the wilderness locale, found earlier in the work of Kenneth Rexroth, this Buddhist perception of oneness, creates a poetry of immediacy and startling originality.

No one can predict with accuracy how the work of this engaging poet, now in his forties, will be received in a future, different era. Will *Myths & Texts* be scrutinized by scholars fifty years from now as are Eliot's "The Waste Land" and Pound's *The Cantos*? Will *Riprap* and *The Back Country*, with their flavor of woodsmoke and snow-melt tea, be read and loved as they are now by a generation learning to travel in the wilderness? Will Snyder's *Mountains and Rivers Without End* be cherished as is Whitman's *Leaves of Grass* as a record of a spiritual journey? And will *Regarding Wave* and *Turtle Island*, pointing to the "power within," continue to energize, as does Blake's poetry, when no fossil fuel is left? No one can say; it is too early to tell.

Nonetheless, it seems that Snyder's works are secure, even if his reputation is, as yet, in flux. After the biographical comment has ceased and when his work is seen in perspective, the dominant voice of Gary Snyder as a poet will become evident. Essentially mystical, Snyder's pre-scientific and mythological perception, grounded in his studies of Buddhism and primitive consciousness, has created a new kind of poetry that is direct, concrete, non-Romantic, and ecological. More than as follower of Pound and Williams, or as a clever adaptor of Oriental poetic forms, Snyder's work will be remembered in its own right as the example of a new direction taken in American literature.

Through Snyder's poems, one senses what archaic religion was all about. As Snyder states, "The primitive world view, far-out scientific knowledge and the poetic imagination are related forces" (*Earth House Hold*, 128). Drawing on these wellsprings, Snyder attempts the creation in his own era of an ecological conscience. And although, as Sherman Paul states, "We cannot expect literature to cure us," it will ". . . hearten us by showing us new and true possibilities and how much may be achieved in life and art by conscious endeavor. Snyder's work . . . does this."[32] Snyder's poetry truly influences one who reads him thoroughly to "see" in a startlingly new way. Presenting the vision of an integrated and unified world, this heroic poetic effort cannot but help to create a much needed change of consciousness.

Notes and References

Chapter One

1. Stated in conversation, by Snyder to Bob Steuding, November 7, 1972.

Chapter Two

1. "Philip Whalen and Gary Snyder," *Poetry U.S.A.* (Bloomington, Indiana, National Educational Television interview, 1965).

2. Kenneth Rexroth, "The New American Poets," *Harper's Magazine*, (June, 1965), p. 67.

3. *Ibid.*

4. Thomas Parkinson, "The Poetry of Gary Snyder," *The Southern Review*, IV (1968), 620.

5. *Riprap, & Cold Mountain Poems* (San Francisco, 1969), p. 15. All references to *Riprap* are taken from this most recent edition. Hereafter, references to Snyder's works will be cited in parentheses in the text following the quotation.

6. Parkinson, p. 624.

7. Stated by Snyder during an open forum on November 7, 1972, at Ulster County Community College, Stone Ridge, New York.

8. All references to *Regarding Wave* are taken from the later edition published by New Directions in 1970.

9. Donald Allen, ed., *The New American Poetry* (New York, 1960), pp. 420–21.

10. Allen, p. 420.

11. David Kherdian, *Six San Francisco Poets* (Fresno, California; 1969), p. 25.

12. Parkinson, pp. 621–22.

13. Charles Altieri, "Gary Snyder's Lyric Poetry: Dialectic as Ecology," *The Far Point*, IV (1970), 62.

14. Robert Graves, *The White Goddess* (New York, 1948).

15. Dom Aelred Graham, *Conversations: Christian and Buddhist* (New York, 1968), p. 76.

16. *Ibid.*

17. *Ibid.*

18. Stephen Berg and Robert Mezey, eds., *Naked Poetry*, (Indianapolis, Indiana; 1969), p. 358.

19. Bruce Cook, *The Beat Generation* (New York, 1971), p. 131.

20. Berg, p. 357.

21. Hyatt H. Waggoner, *American Poets* (Boston, 1968), pp. 615–17.

22. Alfred North Whitehead, *Science and the Modern World* (1926; rpt. Harmondsworth, England, 1938).

23. Paris Leary and Robert Kelly, eds., *A Controversy of Poets* (Garden City, New York; 1965), p. 567.

24. Waggoner, p. 614.

25. Leary, p. 566.

26. Berg, p. 163.

27. *Ibid.*, p. 164.

28. Leary, p. 566.

29. Waggoner, p. 615.

30. *Ibid.*, p. 616.

Chapter Three

1. Waggoner, pp. 331–52. In this regard, also see two articles: Wallace Martin, "The Sources of the Imagist Aesthetic," *Publications of the Modern Language Society*, LXXXV (1970), 196ff. Richard E. Smith, "Ezra Pound and the Haiku," *College English*, XXVI (1965), 522–27.

2. Waggoner, p. 333.

3. *Ibid.*, p. 392.

4. *Ibid.*, pp. 333–34.

5. J. Hillis Miller, *Poets of Reality* (Cambridge, Massachusetts; 1965), p. 7.

6. L. S. Dembo, *Conceptions of Reality in Modern Poetry* (Berkeley, California; 1966), p. 4

7. Edward Sapir, *Language* (New York, 1921). See also Benjamin Lee Whorf, *Language, Thought, and Reality* (Cambridge, Massachusetts; 1956); Susanne K. Langer, *Philosophy in a New Key* (Cambridge, Massachusetts; 1942), pp. 94–127.

8. Miller, pp. 7–8.

9. John R. Carpenter, "Comment," *Poetry*, CXX (1972), 169.

10. Richard Howard, " 'To Hold Both History and Wilderness in Mind': The Poetry of Gary Snyder," *Alone With America: Essays on the Art of Poetry in the United States Since 1950* (New York, 1969), p. 489.

11. Nathaniel Tarn, "From Anthropologist to Informant: A Field Record of Gary Snyder," *Alcheringa: Journal of Ethno-Poetics*, No. 4 (1972), 112.

12. Ezra Pound, *ABC of Reading* (New York, 1960), p. 11.

13. Tarn, p. 112.

14. Wai-lim Yip, *Hiding the Universe: Poems by Wang Wei* (New York, 1972), vii–viii.

15. Allen, p. 421.

16. Archibald MacLeish, *Poetry and Experience* (Boston, 1960), p. 52.

17. Jack Kerouac, *The Dharma Bums* (New York, 1958), p. 17.

18. Ann Charters, ed., *Scenes Along the Road* (New York, 1970), p. 30.

19. Graham, p. 59.

20. Alan Watts, *Beat Zen Square Zen and Zen* (San Francisco, 1959), p. 17

21. Graham, p. 59.

22. Gary Snyder, "On Rinzai Masters and Western Students in Japan," *Wind Bell*, 8, Nos. 1–2 (1969), 27.

23. Philip Kapleau, *The Three Pillars of Zen* (Boston, 1967), pp. 90–91.

24. Thomas Clark, "The Art of Poetry VIII," *Paris Review*, XXXVII (1966), 13–61.

25. Thomas Lyon, "Gary Snyder, a Western Poet," *Western American Literature*, III (1968), 210.

26. For a more detailed study of this aspect of *haiku* see: R. H. Blyth, *Haiku* (Tokyo, Japan; 1949–52), 4 vols.

27. Alan Watts, *The Way of Zen* (New York, 1957), p. 182.

28. *Ibid.*, p. 183.

Chapter Four

1. Letter by Snyder to Bob Steuding, dated May 4, 1973.

2. John R. Swanton, "Tlingit Myths and Texts," *Bureau of American Ethnology*, XXXIX (1909).

3. Allen, p. 421.

4. *Ibid.*

5. Lisel Mueller, "Digging the Universe," *Poetry*, CXI (1968), 255.

6. Henry Seidel Canby, *Thoreau* (Boston, 1939), pp. 40–62.

7. "The Dimensions of a Myth," Bachelor's Thesis, Reed College 1951, pp. 148–49.

8. *Ibid.*, p. 151.

9. *Ibid.*, p. 98.

10. *Ibid.*, p. 96.

11. Joseph Campbell, *The Hero With a Thousand Faces* (Cleveland, Ohio; 1956), p. 30.

12. *Ibid.*, p. 29.

13. Statement made to Bob Steuding by poet Joel Bernstein, July 1970.

14. Letter by Reed Baird dated December, 1972, to Bob Steuding.

15. T. S. Eliot, "Tradition and the Individual Talent," *Selected Essays* (New York, 1950), p. 4.

16. T. S. Eliot, "Notes on 'The Waste Land,'" *The Complete Poems and Plays* (New York, 1952), p. 50.

17. Letter by Snyder dated June 5, 1972, to Bob Steuding.

18. Elizabeth Drew, *T. S. Eliot: The Design of His Poetry* (New York, 1949).

19. "The Dimensions of a Myth," pp. 149–50; quoted from "*Ulysses*, Order and Myth," (1923), rpt. in *Criticism*, Schorer, Miles, and McKenzie, eds. (New York, 1948), p. 270.

20. Robert O. Stephens, "Hemingway and Stendhal: The Matrix of *A Farewell to Arms*," *Publications of the Modern Language Society*, LXXXVIII (1973), 271.

21. T. S. Eliot, *Complete Poems and Plays* (New York, 1952), p. 46, 11. 308–11.

22. Lynn White, Jr., "The Historical Roots of the Ecologic Crisis," *Science*, CLV (1967), 1203–07.

23. Stated in conversation by Snyder November 7, 1972, to Bob Steuding.

24. Parkinson, p. 625.

25. Stated by Snyder during a public reading at Michigan State University, East Lansing, Michigan, May 1, 1969.

26. *Ibid.*

27. The impact in this respect of the ideas of Claude Lévi-Strauss on Snyder's mind is stated by Snyder in Tarn, p. 113.

28. Jaime de Angulo, *Indian Tales* (New York, 1953). Snyder's review appears most recently in *Earth House Hold*, pp. 27–30.

29. Snyder uses Finnish bear mythology gathered on his trip to Stockholm, Sweden, in 1972 in "The Way West Underground" from *Manzanita*. "The Way West Underground" is a sequel to "this poem is for bear" from *Myths & Texts*.

30. A detailed discussion of this subject is to be found in Paul Radin, *The Trickster* (London, 1956).

31. Susanne K. Langer, "Virtual Powers," *Feeling and Form* (New York, 1953).

32. Loren Eiseley, *The Firmament of Time* (New York, 1966), pp. 3–30.

33. Alfred North Whitehead, *Adventures of Ideas* (London, 1933).

34. Altieri, pp. 55–56.

35. *Ibid.*, p. 62.

Chapter Five

1. Allen, p. 421.

2. Kerouac, p. 157.

3. Stated by Snyder in conversation with Bob Steuding, November 7, 1972.

4. Miller Williams, ed., *Contemporary Poetry in America* (New York, 1973), p. 134.

5. Allen, p. 421.

6. Donald Keene, *Japanese Literature* (New York, 1955), pp. 52–53.

7. Arthur Waley, *The Nō Plays of Japan* (New York, 1957), p. 28.

8. *Ibid.*, p. 52.

9. *Ibid.*, p. 36.

10. Allen, p. 421.

11. *Ibid.*

12. "Three Worlds / Three Realms / Six Roads," *Poetry*, CIX (1966), 150. Future page references to this poem will be cited in parentheses in the text.

13. Robert Bly, "The Work of Gary Snyder," *The Sixties*, No. 6 (Spring, 1962), 27–28; 40. Lyon, p. 208.

14. Williams, p. 134.

15. Walt Whitman, *Complete Poetry and Selected Prose*, ed. James E. Miller, Jr. (Boston, 1959), p. 425.

16. *Ibid.*, p. 455.

17. *Ibid.*

18. James E. Miller, Jr., "Walt Whitman and The Secret of History," *Start With the Sun: Studies in the Whitman Tradition*, eds. James E. Miller, Jr. *et al.* (Lincoln, Nebraska, 1960), p. 28.

19. Kapleau, pp. 334–35.

20. Cook, p. 32.

21. Graham, p. 58.

22. Cook, pp. 34–35.

23. Waley, pp. 78–79.

24. *Coyote's Journal*, No. 9 (June, 1971). I have quoted from a copy of this poem kindly forwarded by Gary Snyder.

25. "Philip Whalen and Gary Snyder."

26. Frank Waters, *Book of the Hopi* (New York, 1963), p. 155.

27. "Down," *Iowa Review*, 1, No. 4 (Fall 1970), 85f.

28. "Eight Songs of Clouds and Water," *Poetry*, III (1968), 353.

29. I have worked from a typed copy of this poem, kindly made available to me by Gary Snyder.

30. Bly, p. 28.

31. Snyder refers to himself in a letter to Bob Steuding, dated August 26, 1972, as a "poet-scientist-shaman." At a public forum at Ulster County Community College, Stone Ridge, New York, on November 7, 1972, Snyder referred to Robert Duncan as "the great American shaman poet."

32. Stated by Snyder at a public forum at Ulster County Community College, Stone Ridge, New York on November 7, 1972. For a more detailed discussion of this topic see: Mircea Eliade, *Shamanism: Archaic Techniques of Ecstasy* (New York, 1964).

33. For a more thorough discussion of this historical figure see: René Grousset, *In the Footsteps of the Buddha* (New York, 1971).

34. A discussion of Kokopilau is found in Waters, pp. 45–46.

35. For this insight I am indebted to my friend Joel Bernstein.

36. *Mountains and Rivers Without End Plus One* (San Francisco, 1970), pp. 38–44.

37. *Ibid.*, p. 39.

38. Berg, p. 357.

39. *Mountains and Rivers Without End Plus One*, p. 43.

40. *Ibid.*

41. Stated by Snyder at a public reading at Ulster County Community College, Stone Ridge, New York on November 6, 1972.

Chapter Six

1. For a more detailed discussion of this point see: Bly, pp. 34–36; Lyon, pp. 207–16.

2. Kenneth Rexroth, *The Collected Shorter Poems* (New York, 1966), p. 236.

3. Stated by Snyder in conversation with Bob Steuding, November 6, 1972.

4. Tarn, pp. 111–12.

5. Kenneth Rexroth, *American Poetry in the Twentieth Century* (New York, 1971), p. 177.

6. *Ibid.*, p. 178.

7. "Andree Rexroth," *The Collected Shorter Poems*, p. 154.

8. "Andree Rexroth — Kings River Canyon," *The Collected Shorter Poems*, p. 191. Further page references, quoted in the text, are from this work.

9. Letter by Snyder to Bob Steuding dated June 5, 1972.

10. Henry David Thoreau, "Walking," *Walden and Other Writings*, ed. Brooks Atkinson (New York, 1950), p. 597.

11. Winfield E. Nagley, "Thoreau on Attachment, Detachment, and Non-Attachment," *Philosophy East and West*, III (1954), 307.

12. James Laughlin, ed., *New Directions in Prose and Poetry 23*, (New York, 1971), p. 1.

13. *Ibid.*

14. *Ibid.*, p. 2.

15. *Ibid.*, p. 4.

16. "By Frazier Creek Falls," *Turtle Island* (New York, 1974), p. 41.

17. Thoreau, p. 632.

18. Bly, p. 34.

19. *Ibid.*, p. 35.

20. Parkinson, p. 619.

21. Sherman Paul, *The Shores of America: Thoreau's Inward Exploration* (Urbana, Illinois; 1958), p. 22.

22. Leary, p. 551.

23. *Mountains and Rivers Without End* (San Francisco, 1965), p. 37. All references in this chapter to this work are taken from this edition.

24. "Now, India," *Caterpillar*, 5, No. 3 (1972), 22.

25. *Ibid.*, p. 94.

Chapter Seven

1. Freeman J. Dyson, "Energy in the Universe," in *Energy and Power*, a Scientific American Book (San Francisco, 1971), p. 19.

2. " 'Energy is Eternal Delight,' " *New York Times*, January 12, 1972, p. 43c.

3. Thomas Parkinson, ed., *A Casebook on the Beat* (New York, 1961), p. 155. First published in *Liberation*, IV, 4 (June, 1959), 11.

4. Parkinson, "The Poetry of Gary Snyder," p. 628.

5. "Mother Earth," *New York Times*, July 13, 1972, p. 35.

6. " 'Energy is Eternal Delight.' "

7. William Blake, "The Marriage of Heaven and Hell," *The Complete Writings of William Blake*, ed. Geoffrey Keynes (London, 1957), p. 149.

8. *The White Goddess* (New York, 1948).

9. Parkinson, "The Theory and Practice of Gary Snyder," *Journal of Modern Literature*, 2, No. 3 (1971–72), 451.

10. "Ode: Intimations of Immortality from Recollections of Early Childhood," *Anthology of Romanticism*, 3rd ed., ed. Ernest Bernbaum (New York, 1948), p. 232.

11. Stated by Snyder at a public reading on May 1, 1969, at Michigan State University, East Lansing, Michigan.

12. Gordon Childe, *What Happened in History* (New York, 1946), pp. 41–61; *Man Makes Himself* (New York, 1951), pp. 59–86.

13. G. Devereaux, "The Psychology of Feminine Genital Bleeding," *The International Journal of Psychoanalysis*, 31 (1950), 252–53.

14. Tarn, p. 12.

15. Letter by Snyder to Bob Steuding, dated May 23, 1972.

16. "Philip Whalen and Gary Snyder."

17. D. H. Lawrence, *The Phoenix Edition of D. H. Lawrence* (London, 1955), p. 413.

Chapter Eight

1. Cook, p. 35.

2. Robinson Jeffers, *The Selected Poetry of Robinson Jeffers* (New York, 1938), pp. 588–59.

3. *Ibid.*, p. 197.

4. *Ibid.*, p. 581.

5. Stated by Snyder in conversation with Bob Steuding, November 7, 1972.

6. Letter by Snyder dated May 23, 1972 to Bob Steuding.

7. Jeffers, pp. xiv–xv.

8. Leary, p. 551.

9. Carpenter, p. 168.

10. Alan Brownjohn, "Time & Change," *New Statesman* (December 3, 1971), p. 792.

Chapter Nine

1. Quoted in Don McNeill, *Moving Through Here* (New York, 1970), p. 85.

2. A. T. Baker, "Poetry Today: Low Profile, Flatted Voice," *Time* (July 12, 1971), p. 65.

3. Peter R. Janssen, "By Peter R. Janssen," *Glamour* (May, 1970), p. 177.

4. David Sjostedt, review of *Regarding Wave*, By Gary Snyder, *Rolling Stone* (September 2, 1971, n. p.

5. Lyon, p. 208.

6. Parkinson, "The Poetry of Gary Snyder," p. 620.

7. *Ibid.*, p. 618.

8. Timothy Baland, "A Skipping Stone," *New Republic* (April 4 & 11, 1970), p. 32.

9. Fred Steuding, in conversation with Bob Steuding on December 23, 1971.

10. Aleksandar Nejgebauer, "Observations of an Itinerant Yugoslav: America the Poetical, and Otherwise," *New Republic* (April 26, 1969), p. 22.

11. Parkinson, "The Poetry of Gary Snyder," p. 617.

12. James Dickey, "Five First Books," *Poetry*, XCVII (1961), 316.

13. Bly, pp. 27–28.

14. *Ibid.*, p. 28.

15. *Ibid.*, p. 36.

16. Louis Simpson, quoted in *South Dakota Review*, 5 (Autumn 1967), 18.

17. Robert Sward, "Poetry Chronicle," *Poetry*, XCVI (1960), 246.

18. Thomas Parkinson, "Two Poets," *Prairie Schooner*, XXXIV (Winter, 1960–61), 384.

19. Dell Hymes, review of *Myths & Texts*, by Gary Snyder, *Journal of American Folklore*, LXXIV (April–June, 1961), 184.

20. Lisel Mueller, "Digging the Universe," *Poetry*, III (1968), 254.

21. Richard Howard, " 'To Hold Both History and Wilderness in Mind': The Poetry of Gary Snyder," *Epoch: A Magazine of Contemporary Literature*, XV (Fall, 1965), 88–96.

22. Lyon, pp. 207–16.

23. Parkinson, "The Poetry of Gary Snyder," p. 630.

24. Parkinson, "The Theory and Practice of Gary Snyder," p. 452.

25. Carpenter, p. 168.

26. Roy E. Teele, "Two Poets and Japan," *Poetry*, CXVIII (1971), 174–76.

27. Daniel Jaffe, "A Shared Language in the Poet's Tongue," *Saturday Review* (April 3, 1971), p. 31.

28. Wendel Berry, "A Secular Pilgrimage," *Hudson Review*, XXIII (1970), 423.

29. Altieri, p. 58.

30. Thomas Lyon, "The Ecological Vision of Gary Snyder," *Kansas Quarterly*, II (1970), 117–24.

31. Sherman Paul, "From Lookout to Ashram: The Way of Gary Snyder," *Iowa Review*, I, Nos. 3–4 (Summer and Fall, 1970), 76–91; 70–85.

32. Tom Lewis and Chuck Simmons, "Gary Snyder: A Trilogy," *Mountain Gazette*, XXXVI (August, 1975), 20–28; Alan Williamson, "Gary Snyder: An Appreciation," *The New Republic* (November 1, 1975), pp. 28–30.

33. Paul, "From Lookout to Ashram: The Way of Gary Snyder," p. 85.

Selected Bibliography

PRIMARY SOURCES
(Short publications are omitted)

The Back Country. New York: New Directions, 1968. (First published with translations from Miyazawa Kenji in *A Range of Poems*, this edition contains a significant number of new poems.)

"The Dimensions of a Myth." Portland, Oregon, Reed College Library, June, 1951. (Unpublished bachelor's thesis.)

Earth House Hold. New York: New Directions, 1969. (Snyder's selected prose: journals, reviews, articles.)

The Fudo Trilogy. Berkeley, California: Shaman Drum, 1973.

Manzanita. Bolinas, California: Four Seasons Foundation, 1972.

Myths & Texts. New York: Totem Press, 1960. (Published in association with Corinth Books.)

A Range of Poems. London, England: Fulcrum Press, 1966. (Snyder's collected poems, including translations from Miyazawa Kenji, three of which first appeared in *The East-West Review.*)

Regarding Wave. Iowa City, Iowa: The Windhover Press, 1969. (Limited and signed edition of two hundred eighty copies.)

Regarding Wave. New York: New Directions, 1970. (Adds the sections "Long Hair" and "Target Practice" to the title sequence first published by The Windhover Press.)

Riprap. Ashland, Massachusetts: Origin Press, 1959.

Riprap, & Cold Mountain Poems. San Francisco, California: Four Seasons Foundation, 1965. (Reprint of Origin Press edition of *Riprap*, with translations from Han-shan's "Cold Mountain Poems" first published in *Evergreen Review* added.)

Six Sections from Mountains and Rivers Without End. San Francisco, California: Four Seasons Foundation, 1965.

Six Sections from Mountains and Rivers Without End Plus One. San Francisco, California: Four Seasons Foundation, 1970. (Includes a seventh section, "The Blue Sky." First published in limited edition (1970) by the Phoenix Book Shop.)

Turtle Island. New York: New Directions, 1974.

Anthologies

ALLEN, DONALD M., ed. *The New American Poetry*, 1945–1960. New York: Grove Press, 1960.

BERG, STEPHEN and ROBERT MEZEY, eds. *Naked Poetry: Recent American Poetry in Open Forms*. Indianapolis, Indiana: Bobbs Merrill Co., 1969.

CHACE, JOAN and WILLIAM CHACE. *Making It New*. San Francisco, California: Canfield Press, 1973.

LEARY, PARIS and ROBERT KELLY, eds. *Controversy of Poets: An Anthology of Contemporary American Poetry.* Garden City, New York: Doubleday & Co., 1965.

PARKINSON, THOMAS, ed. *A Casebook on the Beat*. New York: Thomas Y. Crowell Company, 1961.

POULIN, A., JR. *Contemporary American Poetry*. Boston, Massachusetts: Houghton Mifflin Co., 1971.

SECONDARY SOURCES

1. *Bibliographical*

KHERDIAN, DAVID. *A Biographical Sketch and Descriptive Checklist of Gary Snyder*. Berkeley, California: Oyez, 1965. Early spade-work republished in *Six San Francisco Poets*. Fresno, California: The Giligia Press, 1969.

2. *Biographical:* interviews and chapters of books

BARTLETT, LEE. "Gary Snyder," *California Quarterly*, IX (1975), 43–60. Contains a recent interview.

COOK, BRUCE. *The Beat Generation*. New York: Charles Scribner's Sons, 1971. Contains an extensive interview with Snyder of biographical interest.

GRAHAM, DOM AELRED. *Conversations: Christian and Buddhist*. New York: Harcourt, Brace, and World, 1968. Contains a conversation between Snyder and the Catholic priest Graham in Kyoto, Japan, September 4, 1967 concerning Zen and drugs.

MCNEILL, DON. *Moving Through Here*. New York: Alfred Knopf, 1970. Contains a biographical chapter, "Gary Snyder, Doubter of Cities."

Scenes Along the Road, compiled by Ann Charters. New York: Portents/ Gotham Book Mart, 1970. Contains three photographs of Snyder (1955–56) and early comment on Snyder by Allen Ginsberg.

TARN, NATHANIEL. "From Anthropologist to Informant: A Field Record of Gary Snyder," *Alcheringa: Journal of Ethno-Poetics*, No. 4 (1972), pp. 104–14. Interview conducted by poet and anthropologist. Contains significant biographical information.

WATTS, ALAN W. *Beat Zen Square Zen and Zen.* San Francisco, California: City Lights Books, 1959. Pages 16–17 describe Snyder in the early 1950's.

————. *In My Own Way: An Autobiography.* New York: Random House, 1972. High praise for Snyder as a man.

3. *Critical:* articles, reviews, and chapters of books (This section is highly selective.)

ALTIERI, CHARLES. "Gary Snyder's Lyric Poetry: Dialectic as Ecology," *The Far Point,* IV (1970), 55–65. Technical study, discusses Snyder's "ecological intention" and displays its realization in the poem.

BAKER A. T. "Poetry Today: Low Profile, Flatted Voice," *Time,* (July 12, 1971), pp. 64–66. Snyder's work discussed with that of others. Seen as a cult poet.

BALAND, TIMOTHY. "A Skipping Stone," *New Republic,* (April 4 & 11, 1970), pp. 32–33. Discusses the significance of *Earth House Hold* in terms of the contemporary social and political situation.

BERRY, WENDEL. "A Secular Pilgrimage," *Hudson Review,* XXIII (1970), 401–24. Discusses work of Snyder and two other contemporary poets in terms of the tradition of English nature poetry.

BLY, ROBERT. "The Work of Gary Snyder," *The Sixties,* No. 6 (Spring, 1962), pp. 25–42. Important early criticism by a poet-critic; discusses influences and places Snyder within the tradition of Western American writers.

BROWNJOHN, ALAN. "Time & Change," *New Statesman* (December 3, 1971), pp. 791–92. Negative criticism of *Regarding Wave* grounded in an antipathy to Snyder's social philosophy; typical of critics who fail to read Snyder as a poet.

CARPENTER, JOHN R. "Comment," *Poetry,* CXX (June, 1972), 168–69. Review of *Regarding Wave.*

CUSHMAN, JEROME. Review of *The Back Country,* by Gary Snyder. *Library Journal* (April 1, 1968), p. 1488.

DICKEY, JAMES. "Five First Books," *Poetry,* XCVII (February, 1961), 316–20. Praise for *Myths & Texts.* Republished in *The Suspect in Poetry.* Madison, Minnesota: The Sixties Press, 1964.

HAYMAN, RONALD. "From Hart Crane to Gary Snyder," *Encounter,* XXXII (February, 1969), 72–79. Negative criticism from a British publication.

HOWARD, RICHARD. " 'To Hold Both History and Wilderness in Mind': The Poetry of Gary Snyder," *Epoch: A Magazine of Contemporary Literature,* XV (Fall, 1965), 88–96. At times misleading, this article offers valuable insights into *Myths & Texts.* Later expanded and included in Howard's *Alone with America: Essays on the Art of Poetry in the United States Since 1960.* New York: Atheneum Publishers, 1969.

HYMES, DELL H. Review of *Myths & Texts* by Gary Snyder. *Journal of American Folklore*, LXXIV (April–June, 1961), 184. Comment on the work's cultural significance by a noted anthropologist.

JAFFE, DANIEL. "A Shared Language in the Poet's Tongue," *Saturday Review* (April 3, 1971), pp. 31–33; 66. Review of *Regarding Wave*.

KIRBY, DAVID K. "Snyder, Auden, and the New Morality," *Notes on Contemporary Literature*, I (1971), 9–10. Discussion of poets' frank treatment of sex.

LEWIS, TOM and CHUCK SIMMONS. "Gary Snyder: A Trilogy," *Mountain Gazette*, XXXVI (August, 1975), 20–28. Positive and negative criticism of Snyder as poet and public figure.

LYON, THOMAS J. "The Ecological Vision of Gary Snyder," *Kansas Quarterly*, II (1970), 117–24. Timely response relating Snyder's work to the "New Ecology."

———. "Gary Snyder, a Western Poet," *Western American Literature*, III (Fall, 1968), 207–16. Further discussion of Snyder's Western literary imagination, first outlined by Robert Bly.

MUELLER, LISEL. "Digging the Universe," *Poetry*, CXI (January, 1968), 254–56. Review of *A Range of Poems*.

NEJGEBAUER, ALEKSANDAR. "Observations of an Itinerant Yugoslav: America the Poetical, and Otherwise," *New Republic* (April 26, 1969), pp. 19–24. Casual negative criticism of Snyder and his social philosophy.

PARKINSON, THOMAS. "After the Beat Generation," *Colorado Quarterly*, (Summer, 1968), 45–56. Study of the post-Beat movement with considerable emphasis on Snyder.

———. "The Poetry of Gary Snyder," *The Southern Review*, IV (1968), 616–32. Balanced and insightful criticism covering Snyder's work from *Riprap* through *The Back Country*. Important article.

———. "The Theory and Practice of Gary Snyder," *Journal of Modern Literature*, II, 3 (1971–72), 448–52. Discusses the stylistic and philosophical development of Snyder as evidenced in *Earth House Hold* and *Regarding Wave*.

———. "Two Poets," *Prairie Schooner*, XXXIV (Winter, 1960–61), 383–86. Early review of *Myths & Texts*.

PAUL, SHERMAN. "From Lookout to Ashram: The Way of Gary Snyder," *Iowa Review*, I, 3–4 (Summer & Fall, 1970), 76–91; 70–85. Discusses Snyder's evolving radicalism, from passivism and withdrawal to activism and communitarianism.

"Poetry: Combatting Society With Surrealism," *Time*, 24 January 1969, p. 73. *The Back Country* is reviewed briefly with eleven other volumes of poetry.

REXROTH, KENNETH. *American Poetry in the Twentieth Century*. New York: Herder and Herder, 1971. Snyder as elegiac poet.

————. "A Hope for Poetry," *Holiday* (March, 1966), pp. 147–51. Snyder given praise by older poet.

————. "The New American Poets," *Harper's Magazine*, CCXXX (June, 1965), 65–71. Snyder receives prominent mention.

ROSENTHAL , M. L. *The New Poets.* New York: Oxford University Press, 1967. Contains favorable mention of Snyder's work.

ROSS, NANCY WILSON. "Allen Ginsberg as Winnie-the-Pooh, Gary Snyder as Japhy Ryder," *New York Times Book Review*, May 11, 1969, pp. 8; 10. Review of *Earth House Hold;* discusses Snyder as culture-hero.

ROSZAK, THEODORE. "Technocracy: Despotism of Beneficent Expertise," *Nation* (September 1, 1969), p. 182. Negative criticism of *Earth House Hold* from the perspective of a contemporary social critic.

SCOTT, ROBERT IAN. "Gary Snyder's Early Uncollected Mallory Poem," *Concerning Poetry*, II (1969), 33–37. The publication with a critical introduction of one of Snyder's early poems, written in 1950 while at Reed College.

SIMPSON, LOUIS. "New Books of Poems," *Harper's Magazine* (August 1968), p. 76. Negative criticism of *The Back Country.*

STEUDING, BOB. "The Child of the Mountain God," *Michigan State News*, "Collage," (April 22, 1969), pp. 9; 12. Biographical sketch and overview of criticism.

SWARD, ROBERT W. "Poetry Chronicle," *Poetry*, XCVI (July, 1960), 244–46. First major criticism of *Riprap.*

TEELE, ROY E. "Two Poets and Japan," *Poetry*, CXVIII (June, 1971), 174–76. Discusses the influence of the Japanese travel diary on *Earth House Hold.*

WAGGONER, HYATT H. *American Poets.* Boston, Massachusetts: Houghton Mifflin, 1968. Mentions Zen influence.

WILLIAMSON, ALAN. "Gary Snyder: An Appreciation," *The New Republic*, (November 1, 1975), pp. 28–30. Laudatory response to Snyder's winning the Pulitzer Prize for Poetry for 1975.

ZAHNISER, EDWARD. "Poet in Today's Wilderness," *Living Wilderness*, XXXIII (Spring, 1969), 34–36. Presents Snyder's poetry, especially *The Back Country*, and its relevance to the conservation movement.

Index

PS3569
N88Z9   **Steuding, Bob.**
         E24974   7.95
         Gary Snyder / by Bob Steuding. — Boston : Twayne, c197(
         189 p. : port. ; 21 cm. - (Twayne's United States authors series ; TUSAS 27-
         Bibliography: p 178-182.
         Includes index
         ISBN 0-8057-7174-3

              1. Snyder, Gary—Criticism and interpretation.

         PS3569.N88Z9   811'.5'4   76-1493
                                          [B]   MAR

         Library of Congress   76